An Analysis of

Aristotle's

Metaphysics

T0301895

Aiste Celkyte

Routledge
Taylor & Francis Group

LONDON AND NEW YORK

Published by Macat International Ltd
24:13 Coda Centre, 189 Munster Road, London SW6 6AW.

Distributed exclusively by Routledge
2 Park Square, Milton Park, Abingdon, Oxon OX14 4RN
605 Third Avenue, New York, NY 10017

Routledge is an imprint of the Taylor & Francis Group, an informa business

www.macat.com
info@macat.com

Cataloguing in Publication Data
A catalogue record for this book is available from the British Library.
Library of Congress Cataloguing-in-Publication Data is available upon request.
Cover illustration: Etienne Gilfillan

ISBN 978-1-912302-95-6 (hardback)
ISBN 978-1-912127-21-4 (paperback)
ISBN 978-1-912281-83-1 (e-book)

Notice
The information in this book is designed to orientate readers of the work under analysis,
to elucidate and contextualise its key ideas and themes, and to aid in the development
of critical thinking skills. It is not meant to be used, nor should it be used, as a
substitute for original thinking or in place of original writing or research. References and
notes are provided for informational purposes and their presence does not constitute
endorsement of the information or opinions therein. This book is presented solely for
educational purposes. It is sold on the understanding that the publisher is not engaged
to provide any scholarly advice. The publisher has made every effort to ensure that
this book is accurate and up-to-date, but makes no warranties or representations with
regard to the completeness or reliability of the information it contains. The information
and the opinions provided herein are not guaranteed or warranted to produce particular
results and may not be suitable for students of every ability. The publisher shall not be
liable for any loss, damage or disruption arising from any errors or omissions, or from
the use of this book, including, but not limited to, special, incidental, consequential or
other damages caused, or alleged to have been caused, directly or indirectly, by the
information contained within.

CONTENTS

THE MACAT LIBRARY

The Macat Library is a series of unique academic explorations of seminal works in the humanities and social sciences – books and papers that have had a significant and widely recognised impact on their disciplines. It has been created to serve as much more than just a summary of what lies between the covers of a great book. It illuminates and explores the influences on, ideas of, and impact of that book. Our goal is to offer a learning resource that encourages critical thinking and fosters a better, deeper understanding of important ideas.

Each publication is divided into three Sections: Influences, Ideas, and Impact. Each Section has four Modules. These explore every important facet of the work, and the responses to it.

This Section-Module structure makes a Macat Library book easy to use, but it has another important feature. Because each Macat book is written to the same format, it is possible (and encouraged!) to cross-reference multiple Macat books along the same lines of inquiry or research. This allows the reader to open up interesting interdisciplinary pathways.

To further aid your reading, lists of glossary terms and people mentioned are included at the end of this book (these are indicated by an asterisk [*] throughout) – as well as a list of works cited.

Macat has worked with the University of Cambridge to identify the elements of critical thinking and understand the ways in which six different skills combine to enable effective thinking.
Three allow us to fully understand a problem; three more give us the tools to solve it. Together, these six skills make up the **PACIER** model of critical thinking. They are:

ANALYSIS – understanding how an argument is built
EVALUATION – exploring the strengths and weaknesses of an argument
INTERPRETATION – understanding issues of meaning

CREATIVE THINKING – coming up with new ideas and fresh connections
PROBLEM-SOLVING – producing strong solutions
REASONING – creating strong arguments

To find out more, visit **WWW.MACAT.COM.**

CRITICAL THINKING AND *METAPHYSICS*

Primary critical thinking skill: REASONING
Secondary critical thinking skill: ANALYSIS, INTERPRETATION, EVALUATION

Aristotle's *Metaphysics* is a collection of essays on a wide range of topics, almost certainly never put together by Aristotle himself. This helps to explain why the material covers such a very wide range of material, from meaning to mathematics, from logical sequences to religion. It includes very useful treatments of the nature of axioms (or primary truths) such as the law of non-contradiction and the laws of logic.

In looking at these, Aristotle provides sustained guides to clear thinking as would be evidenced in analysis and evaluation of arguments and the production of good reasoning. He also provides some valuable discussion of interpretation by looking at homonyms (as in 'this knife is sharp' and 'this note is sharp') and what he calls 'paronyms,' which lie between homonyms and synonyms: an example is the word 'healthy'. *Metaphysics* is also useful to study for its frequent examples of hypothetical reasoning, including their use in mathematics ('if x, then y…') and science ('if a moves b, then b moves c...', so what moves a?). In addition, we find Aristotle analysing Plato's arguments and subjecting them to sustained (critical) evaluation. While *Metaphysics* shows Aristotle in many well-developed critical thinking modes, it is first and foremost a work of exquisite reasoning, creating strong arguments that continue to be debated and deployed today, nearly 2500 years after they were written.

ABOUT THE AUTHOR OF THE ORIGINAL WORK

Aristotle was born in 384 BCE in what is present-day Macedonia. At the age of 17, he moved to Athens in Greece to begin an education in philosophy under Plato, one of the founders of European philosophy, at his renowned Academy. On Plato's death in 347 BCE, Aristotle moved back to Macedonia to tutor the young Alexander the Great. But in 335 BCE he returned to Athens and established his own school, the Lyceum. Political unrest forced Aristotle to leave Athens again in 322 BCE, and he died shortly afterwards on the island of Euboea.

ABOUT THE AUTHOR OF THE ANALYSIS

Dr Aiste Celkyte is a researcher specialising in ancient philosophy. She is currently a postdoctoral researcher at Yonsei University in South Korea.

ABOUT MACAT

GREAT WORKS FOR CRITICAL THINKING

Macat is focused on making the ideas of the world's great thinkers accessible and comprehensible to everybody, everywhere, in ways that promote the development of enhanced critical thinking skills.

It works with leading academics from the world's top universities to produce new analyses that focus on the ideas and the impact of the most influential works ever written across a wide variety of academic disciplines. Each of the works that sit at the heart of its growing library is an enduring example of great thinking. But by setting them in context – and looking at the influences that shaped their authors, as well as the responses they provoked – Macat encourages readers to look at these classics and game-changers with fresh eyes. Readers learn to think, engage and challenge their ideas, rather than simply accepting them.

'Macat offers an amazing first-of-its-kind tool for interdisciplinary learning and research. Its focus on works that transformed their disciplines and its rigorous approach, drawing on the world's leading experts and educational institutions, opens up a world-class education to anyone.'

Andreas Schleicher
Director for Education and Skills, Organisation for Economic Co-operation and Development

'Macat is taking on some of the major challenges in university education … They have drawn together a strong team of active academics who are producing teaching materials that are novel in the breadth of their approach.'

Prof Lord Broers,
former Vice-Chancellor of the University of Cambridge

'The Macat vision is exceptionally exciting. It focuses upon new modes of learning which analyse and explain seminal texts which have profoundly influenced world thinking and so social and economic development. It promotes the kind of critical thinking which is essential for any society and economy.
This is the learning of the future.'

Rt Hon Charles Clarke, former UK Secretary of State for Education

'The Macat analyses provide immediate access to the critical conversation surrounding the books that have shaped their respective discipline, which will make them an invaluable resource to all of those, students and teachers, working in the field.'

Professor William Tronzo, University of California at San Diego

WAYS IN TO THE TEXT

KEY POINTS

- Born in 384 B.C.E., Aristotle spent most of his life in Athens,* Greece, where he studied with Plato,* established his own school, and wrote his works. He died in 322 B.C.E.

- *Metaphysics* challenged long-established philosophical theories about the nature of being, including those of Aristotle's teacher, Plato.

- Much of the history of philosophy has involved debate about the relative merits of Plato's and Aristotle's theories. While neither can claim absolute relevance today, Aristotle's work still provides intellectual food for thought for new generations of philosophers.

Who Was Aristotle?

Born in the Greek city of Stageira in 384 B.C.E., Aristotle became one of the most important teachers and philosophers of the ancient world. His father, a court doctor in Macedonia* (on the northern edges of Classical Greece), taught him biology and empirical* studies, that is the means of gaining knowledge based on observation or experience. At the age of 17, Aristotle moved to Athens and joined the Academy,* the school founded by the renowned philosopher Plato. He studied there until Plato's death in 347 B.C.E. Plato had himself studied with the great philosopher Socrates,* which gave Aristotle access to the prime philosophical wisdom of the era.

After Plato died, Aristotle returned to the Macedonian court and became the tutor of a nine-year-old boy named Alexander. The child would grow up to become one of the most powerful rulers of the ancient world: Alexander the Great.* Aristotle tutored Alexander until the boy turned 16. In 335 B.C.E., Aristotle returned to Athens and established his own school, the Lyceum.* He wrote most of his key works—including *Metaphysics*—while he was there. He left Athens again in 322 B.C.E. and died later that year.

Unfortunately, very little of Aristotle's work survives. In fact, his reputation faded not long after his death and it was not until around three centuries later, when a Roman editor named Andronicus* collected and published Aristotle's essays, that his work became central to the study of philosophy. The book's title, *Metaphysics*, even gave a name to the philosophical discipline dedicated to studying the fundamental nature of being. But Aristotle died long before his editor coined the word metaphysics,* and the editor may have meant it to signify nothing more than the book's placement in Aristotle's body of work—that it came after (the Greek word *meta*) his work entitled *Physics*.

What Does *Metaphysics* Say?

For centuries before Aristotle, thinkers pursuing ontology*—the study of the nature of being—had theorized about what "being" actually is. Earlier philosophers had suggested that "substance"*—the thing that underlies all existence—was the air. Another thought it was water. A third thought fire. Yet another decided substance was, in fact, a combination of four elements, adding "earth" to the mix. Then in the fourth century B.C.E., Aristotle's teacher Plato changed the discussion forever when he theorized that eternal, bodiless "forms" existing independently in the world create the realities we perceive. This became known as Plato's Theory of Forms.*

Despite the fact that he had studied with Plato, Aristotle did not hesitate to disagree with his teacher's conclusions. Abandoning the notion of bodiless (or incorporeal)* forms, Aristotle suggested that form only exists when it is present in matter. He pointed out a logical inconsistency in Plato's theory. If every object requires a form to copy so that it may come into existence, then a man must have a "form" of a man to copy. And where does that form come from? This has become known as the "third man"* argument.

Aristotle primarily aims to investigate what he calls "being qua being"*—"qua" meaning "by virtue of what is." But in the loose collection of ideas that make up *Metaphysics*, other subjects arise as well. Aristotle also tackles concepts such as "potentiality" and "actuality,"* using them to answer a philosophical question that the philosopher Parmenides* had raised over a century earlier. Essentially, Parmenides' complex argument made the case that because there is no such thing as a state of non-being, change is essentially impossible. Aristotle disagreed with that argument by making a distinction between being-as-potential and being-as-actuality. A child exists both as a potential adult and as an actual child. In Aristotle's view, change did not involve the transformation from a state of non-being to being but from a state of potentiality into one of actuality.

Another important argument Aristotle developed in *Metaphysics* is the theory of the "unmoved mover"*—a kind of heavenly catalyst that serves as the source of all movement in the world. Are there many unmoved movers or only one? Aristotle's conclusions remain unclear, as he makes a case for each idea in different books in *Metaphysics*.

Supporting his theories through his strong analytical skills and powers of observation, Aristotle accepted some previous scholarship while overturning long-held beliefs about the nature of existence. He also raised a host of new questions for future philosophers to deal with—part of the reason his work remained central to the discipline of philosophy for so long. Subsequent generations of philosophers would continue to debate the merits of Platonic* versus Aristotelian interpretations. In some ways, the debates inspired by Aristotle's thought continue today and Aristotle's reputation as one of the founding minds of philosophy remains unquestioned.

Why Does *Metaphysics* Matter?

In *Metaphysics*, Aristotle tackled a subject that philosophers had been debating for centuries before him: what is "being"? While that question remains central to the study of metaphysics, the answers Aristotle offered nearly two thousand years ago continue to be relevant to the discussion.

While a number of Aristotle's works have survived, even if he had written nothing but *Metaphysics* his reputation would be assured. His work has influenced philosophers throughout the centuries—from the ancient Greeks of his day to the Romans,* to medieval* philosophers in Christian* and Islamic* cultures, all the way to the present day. Twelfth-century Islamic philosopher Averroes (Ibn Rushd)* and Christian cleric Thomas Aquinas* in the thirteenth century both used Aristotelian concepts in their work. In the eighteenth century, Scottish philosopher David Hume*—whose philosophy held, in essence, that one cannot know anything for certain without evidence—criticized Aristotle for having drawn unsupported conclusions about substance. After Hume, Aristotle's influence began to decline. But nevertheless, his works remained a part of the academic curriculum, as they do today.

In the second half of the twentieth century, philosophers revived their interest in metaphysics. The concerns metaphysicians address today differ from those considered in Aristotle's time, but scholars still recognize the historical and philosophical importance of his work. Some study *Metaphysics* and his other works exegetically*—that is, analyzing and interpreting the text to try to get to Aristotle's original meaning. Others look to this ancient text as a source of fresh inspiration. These scholars adapt Aristotle's thinking to the present day and seek to expand on his insights. For instance, Aristotle's ideas about the difference between substantial properties* and accidental properties* has inspired the modern theory of essentialism.* Essentialism holds that every entity has certain core attributes that constitute its identity and function. As the essentialist theory challenges Hume, in a sense we have come full circle. Hume refuted Aristotle; Aristotelian thinking refutes Hume.

British philosopher Jonathan Barnes* noted that "an account of Aristotle's intellectual afterlife would be little less than a history of European thought."[1] As we seem to be in the midst of a revival of interest in Aristotle's work today, that afterlife continues.

NOTES

1   Jonathan Barnes, *A Very Short Introduction to Aristotle* (Oxford: Oxford University Press, 2000), 136.

SECTION 1
INFLUENCES

MODULE 1
THE AUTHOR AND THE
HISTORICAL CONTEXT

KEY POINTS

- *Metaphysics* is one of the most important works in the history of its philosophical discipline.

- The time Aristotle spent in Athens* among other philosophers greatly influenced his work.

- Plato's* mentorship was especially important for the development of Aristotle's thought.

Why Read This Text?

One of the most important works of ancient philosophy, Aristotle's *Metaphysics* consists of 14 treatises, named after letters of the Greek alphabet, which address various metaphysical topics. In fact, the name of the philosophical subfield of metaphysics* comes from the title of this book.

Metaphysics asks the central question: what is substance?* As philosophy professor Christopher Shields* explains, in this work Aristotle argues that, "it is … possible to study all beings insofar as they are related to the core instance of being, and then also to study that core instance, namely substance."[1] Aristotle most prominently addresses the question of substance in book Zeta of *Metaphysics*. The other books contain discussions more or less pertinent to this topic as well, but they focus mostly on other issues. Examples of this are as follows:

- The explanation and assessment of philosophical thinking in the time before the Greek philosopher Socrates* (an era known as pre-Socratic).*

❝ Aristotle was born, 15 years after Socrates' death, in the small colony of Stagira, on the peninsula of Chalcidice. He was the son of Nicomachus, court physician to King Amyntas, the grandfather of Alexander the Great. After the death of his father he migrated to Athens in 367, being then 17, and joined Plato's Academy. He remained for 20 years as Plato's pupil and colleague, and it can safely be said that on no other occasion in history was such intellectual power concentrated in a single institution. ❞

Anthony Kenny, *Ancient Philosophy: A New History of Western Philosophy*

- A critique of the philosopher Plato's Theory of Forms*—that non-material forms or ideas rather than the material world we know through our sensations are most fundamentally real.
- Relationships between parts and wholes—the study of parts and wholes concerns such questions as whether there are composite objects (complex objects with sub-parts) whose existence consists of more than *just* the sum of their parts.

Among the more famous ideas Aristotle presents in *Metaphysics* are the discussion of the nature of change and the idea that the first cause of all change in the universe is an unmoved mover.* This unmoved mover moves other things, but is not itself moved by any previous action.

Aristotle's analysis of these topics greatly influenced the debates on metaphysics in antiquity* (the period before the Middle Ages,* but within the span of Western human history), the Middle Ages, and beyond, even to the present day. Anyone who wishes to study the history of philosophical thought or to investigate central metaphysical questions more generally would do well to begin with *Metaphysics*.

Author's Life

Born in 384 B.C.E. in the Greek city of Stageira, Aristotle learned biology and empirical* studies (gaining knowledge based on experience or observation) from his father, a court doctor in Macedonia.* The most important stage in Aristotle's education, however, came when he moved to Athens and joined Plato's school, the Academy,* in 367 B.C.E. He remained there until Plato's death in 347 B.C.E.

After leaving the Academy, Aristotle tutored future king and warrior Alexander the Great* in Macedonia. Returning to Athens in 335 B.C.E., he established the Lyceum,* his own philosophical school, and here he wrote all his major works, including *Metaphysics*. "This second period of residency in Athens was an astonishingly productive one for Aristotle ... many of the philosophical works of Aristotle that we possess today probably derive from this period."[2]

As with most ancient philosophers, we know little about the details of Aristotle's life. But the rich intellectual culture of Athens surely played a key role in the development of his thought.

Athens was a significant political center. Aristotle would have been able to develop his political thoughts by watching politics firsthand. As for the study of metaphysics, Athens provided an environment in which a thinker such as Aristotle would not just be introduced to a variety of philosophical concepts, but would also observe these ideas being put to the test through philosophical debates. His education therefore meant that he became well acquainted with the ideas that he later criticized and rejected in *Metaphysics*. The most important of these was Plato's Theory of Forms.

Author's Background

Despite being a well-known member of the philosophical community, Aristotle had limited social status, because he was not a full citizen of Athens. As a resident alien—a "metic"* in Greek—he could not fully participate in the political life of Athens, could not own land, and had to pay higher taxes than a full citizen. We can only speculate on this, but it might have been his metic status that led him to leave Athens after Plato's death. Scholar Jonathan Barnes* describes one possible scenario: "In 347 the northern town of Olynthus has just fallen to the Macedonian army, and the anti-Macedonian party in Athens, led by the orator Demosthenes,* was in the ascendant. Aristotle was not— then or ever—an Athenian citizen, and this situation may have been delicate."[3] The reappearance of anti-Macedonian feeling 25 years later caused him to leave Athens again at the very end of his life.[4]

Although the restrictions placed on a resident alien must have affected Aristotle in some way, his work does not reflect this. His intellectual surroundings were exceptionally favorable for philosophical activities. Aristotle spent 20 years in Plato's Academy and Plato was himself a pupil of Socrates. As philosophy professor Anthony Kenny* notes, "… it can safely be said that on no other occasion in history was such intellectual power concentrated in a single institution."[5]

NOTES

1 Christopher Shields, "Aristotle," *Stanford Encyclopedia of Philosophy*, accessed February 10, 2015, http://plato.stanford.edu/entries/aristotle/.

2 Christopher Shields, "Aristotle's Philosophical Life and Writing," in *The Oxford Handbook of Aristotle*, ed. Christopher Shields (Oxford: Oxford University Press, 2012), 8.

3 Jonathan Barnes, "Life and work," in *The Cambridge Companion to Aristotle*, ed. Jonathan Barnes (Cambridge: Cambridge University Press, 1995), 4–5.

4 Barnes, "Life and work," 6.

5 Anthony Kenny, *Ancient Philosophy: A New History of Western Philosophy* (Oxford: Oxford University Press, 2006), 65.

MODULE 2
ACADEMIC CONTEXT

KEY POINTS

- The field of metaphysics* addresses the questions pertinent to existence and reality or, according to Aristotle's famous claim, "being qua being"*—being by virtue of being.
- Pre-Socratic* philosophers had all analyzed the topic of fundamental existence, as had Aristotle's teacher Plato.*
- Aristotle made significant contributions to the development of metaphysical tradition.

The Work in its Context

Aristotle did not title his work *Metaphysics*. Some three centuries after his death, a Roman editor named Andronicus* collected the essays that make up the book and gave them this title. Why? A common explanation is that Andronicus intended to show that this work came after Aristotle's writing on physics. The literal meaning of the Greek phrase *meta ta physica* is "after the physics."

But thanks to Andronicus, the subfield of philosophy that Aristotle's work spawned has been named after it. Broadly speaking, the discipline of metaphysics addresses questions about existence, reality, or being itself. Aristotle wrote, "There is a science which investigates being as being ... Now this is not the same as any of the so-called special sciences; for none of these others deals generally with being as being."[1] Studying "being qua being" became a defining concept for metaphysics. It is best understood in this way: "The science is in some sense wholly general or universal, for it is contrasted with the special sciences, each of which 'cuts off' a portion of reality and studies it ...

66 In searching for explanation, men inevitably
encounter difficulties ... These difficulties are, for
Aristotle, the starting point of philosophy. It is by
working one's way through the puzzles or difficulties
that philosophical wisdom grows. Hence Aristotle
devotes an entire book of the *Metaphysics* simply to
cataloguing the puzzles surrounding the question of
what are the basic elements of reality. 99

Jonathan Lear, *Aristotle: The Desire to Understand*

Our science, on the other hand,—or metaphysics ... —deals with
beings in general."[2] Ever since Aristotle's time, metaphysics has
referred to the study of problems concerning the fundamental
existence or being, as opposed to studies dedicated to specific objects
or phenomena.

Overview of the Field

Aristotle's *Metaphysics* defined its field in many ways. But it also has
roots in previous philosophical tradition. As Aristotle himself notes in
book Alpha of *Metaphysics*, many Greek philosophers before him
engaged in the questions of ontology*—studying the nature of being.
English philosopher Anthony Kenny* notes that, "most dissertations
that begin with literature searches seek to show that all work hitherto
has left a gap that will now be filled by the author's original research.
Aristotle's *Metaphysics* is no exception ... The earliest philosophy, he
concluded, is, on all subjects, full of babble, since in its beginnings it is
but an infant."[3]

Most of the thinkers Aristotle counts as his predecessors were pre-
Socratic philosophers. An especially important group of pre-Socratics
was the Milesian* school, which took its name from Miletus, the town
where it originated. As one introduction to ancient philosophy says,

"The first pre-Socratics, Thales,* Anaximander,* and Anaximenes*— from Miletus in Asia Minor—were concerned to provide cosmologies,* reasoned accounts of the world we live in. As Aristotle acutely saw, they focused on what he called the material cause—the question of what our world is composed of."[4]

Aristotle found the scope of the ideas put forward by Milesians to be limited. But he did not always criticize them. He was positively impressed by other pre-Socratics such as Empedocles.* "Aristotle praised him for realizing that a cosmological theory must not just identify the elements of the universe, but must assign causes for the development and intermingling of the elements to make the living and inanimate compounds of the actual world."[5] Pre-Socratic ideas, therefore, provided a rich intellectual soil in which Aristotle could develop his own views.

Academic Influences

Little evidence survives about Aristotle's intellectual life in general and the information we have can be contradictory. One of the questions on which sources disagree is the relationship between Aristotle and the previous intellectual tradition. One line of scholarship paints Aristotle as an especially arrogant person, condescending to both his contemporaries and earlier philosophers. The other line of scholarship says that Aristotle respected and cared about his friends and colleagues. Scholar Christopher Shields* concludes that, "we should simply admit what is plain: the negative remarks in the ancient biographical tradition surrounding Aristotle are mainly the views of his enemies, men driven by petty jealousy and competitive zeal rather than by a sober interest in neutral assessment."[6]

Aristotle's most important influence was probably his teacher Plato. Aristotle studied in Plato's Academy* for two decades, so it stands to reason that his intellectual relationship with the elder philosopher shaped his own development. That is not to say Aristotle embraced Plato's ideas wholeheartedly. Aristotle is known for criticizing Platonic* ideas. Although we cannot say exactly how Plato influenced Aristotle, it is clear that on the whole he was a positive influence.

Scholar Jonathan Barnes* argued that, "there are centrally Aristotelian texts for which Plato's views are evidently a main source of inspiration and of puzzlement (thus the last two books of the *Metaphysics* are largely moved by Platonic notions about mathematics) and—more vaguely but more importantly—whole areas of Aristotle's philosophical interests were shaped and determined by Plato's philosophical interests."[7]

NOTES

1   Aristotle, *Metaphysics*, trans. William David Ross, in *The Complete Works of Aristotle: The Revised Oxford Translation*, ed. Jonathan Barnes (Princeton, NJ: Princeton University Press, 1984), 2:1584.

2   Jonathan Barnes, "Metaphysics," in *The Cambridge Companion to Aristotle*, ed. Jonathan Barnes (Cambridge: Cambridge University Press, 1995), 69.

3   Anthony Kenny, *Ancient Philosophy: A New History of Western Philosophy* (Oxford: Oxford University Press, 2006), 3.

4   Julia Annas, *Ancient Philosophy: A Very Short Introduction* (Oxford: Oxford University Press, 2000), 100.

5   Kenny, *Ancient Philosophy*, 22.

6   Christopher Shields, *Aristotle* (London: Routledge, 2007), 15.

7   Jonathan Barnes, "Life and work," in *The Cambridge Companion to Aristotle*, ed. Jonathan Barnes (Cambridge: Cambridge University Press, 1995), 17–18.

MODULE 3
THE PROBLEM

KEY POINTS

- In the period when *Metaphysics* was conceived, philosophers generally engaged with questions relating to the fundamental principles of existence.

- A little before Aristotle's time, while his teacher Plato* was developing his Theory of Forms,* pre-Socrates* questioned the functioning of the natural world.

- Aristotle's work engages with the previous philosophical tradition both by using concepts created by earlier thinkers and by criticizing some of their views and approaches.

Core Question

Long before Aristotle wrote *Metaphysics*, one of the issues stirring heated debate among philosophers was the question of substance.* As Aristotle himself notes in book Zeta of *Metaphysics*, "the question which, both now and of old, has always been raised, and always been the subject of doubt, viz. what being is, is just the question, what is substance?"[1]

The philosophical notion of substance can be difficult to grasp as it has many nuances, but its core meaning remains relatively uncomplicated. We can best understand substances as "ontologically* basic entities:"[2] that is, a substance is the essence of an object, as opposed to any accidental properties* the object might have. For example, those who believe in substance theory say the substance of a person is distinct from physical attributes, such as being pale-skinned or having a snub nose. The notion of a substance depicts the very fundamental parts of an object's existence. Aristotle even claims that, "substance is a principle and a cause."[3]

> ❝ And indeed the question which, both now and of
> old, has always been raised, and always been the subject
> of doubt, viz. what being is, is just the question, what is
> substance? ❞
>
> Aristotle, *Metaphysics*

The interest in fundamental existence goes back to the early pre-Socratic thinkers such as Thales,* Anaximander,* and Anaximenes.* They discussed the principles of how the world functions. Each of the pre-Socratics had a different idea about which natural element was responsible for the reality we experience. Thales, for instance, claimed that water is the primary principle underlying all existence. Anaximenes disagreed, arguing that it was air, while Anaximander proposed the existence of apeiron,* a special "limitless" element that generated the world. Later pre-Socratics continued this tradition. Heraclitus* argued that the world is governed by a principle based on rationality (logos),* which he also called fire. Empedocles,* meanwhile, was the first philosopher to introduce the theory of the four elements together (fire, water, earth, air).

Discussions about ontology—the study of the nature of being—changed dramatically in the Athens of the fourth century B.C.E., when Aristotle's teacher, Plato, introduced the notion of non-bodily forms as the causes of existence. In what are known as his middle dialogues, Plato presented the argument that incorporeal,* eternal, independently existing forms account for all reality. This theory turned out to be a game changer in metaphysical* debates in general, and an important innovation in debates on the nature of substance.

The Participants

Plato's metaphysics holds a very significant place in the history of philosophy in its own right. But it also provides an essential key to understanding Aristotle's position. Arguably Plato's most significant innovation was his Theory of Forms. This theory supposes that forms exist as causal entities.

In simpler terms, Plato's work makes a distinction between "being" and "becoming." While "becoming" describes the constantly changing, perishable, and unstable actual world, the forms—referred to as "being"—always stay the "same and in the same state."[4] The forms, moreover, act as causes of properties in the world of becoming. Plato saw objects in the world of becoming as partaking* in the forms. In this way, things in the actual world represent their respective forms, while at the same time, they are also "copies" or things derived from the forms. But forms are not derived from anything else. So Plato often states that only they—the forms—belong to the reality of true being.[5] A beautiful person, for instance, is beautiful by virtue of partaking in the form of beauty. This form constitutes what "beautiful" is, while the person is a kind of reflection of the form.

This complex theory has many implications. As British philosopher and academic Verity Harte* explains, "Forms have a role to play in Plato's theory of being or what there is: 1. Forms are (among the primary) beings. 2. Further … Forms are identified as having causal responsibility for things other than Forms having some of the character they do; the Form of beauty, for example, has causal responsibility for the beauty of anything else that is beautiful. In this way, Forms are not only themselves beings, they are causally responsible for at least certain other aspects of the character of the world, as well."[6] For this reason, "Forms are Plato's substances, for everything derives its existence from Forms."[7]

The Contemporary Debate

Aristotle criticizes Plato's ideas about substance throughout *Metaphysics*, and especially in books Zeta, Mu, and Nu. Aristotle's critique concentrates on Plato's idea that forms are both incorporeal (bodiless), eternal, independently existing entities and the causes of existence. According to Plato's view, an object becomes beautiful by partaking in the form of beauty, which represents perfect beauty and the origin of all the beauty in the world. This means that properties derive from forms. Aristotle saw things differently: "If, then, we view the matter from these standpoints, it is plain that no universal* attribute is a substance, and this is plain also from the fact that no common predicate indicates a 'this', but rather a 'such'. If not, many difficulties follow and especially the 'third man.'"[8] Aristotle's third man argument* contends that if Plato's forms cause existence, then these forms themselves need other forms in order to exist. For example, a man exists as a man by assuming the form of man. However, in order for this man's form to exist, there must be a form of a form of man—the third man—and so on.

Aristotle suggests that when discussing substances, we ought to be talking about objects themselves rather than their accidental properties. In his own theory, Aristotle discards the notion of incorporeal and eternal forms. He does use the notion of form, but in a rather different way from Plato. He writes, "by form I mean the essence of each thing and its primary substance."[9] Form, according to Aristotle, is immanent,* that is, it only exists when it is present in matter. But it is important to note the formulation. Substance is "form present in matter," but not a *compound* of form and matter. Aristotle rejects the latter option, because compounds cannot be primary.[10] This philosophically rigorous and innovative idea made Aristotle one of the most important metaphysicians in the history of philosophy.

NOTES

1   Aristotle, Metaphysics, trans. William David Ross, in *The Complete Works of Aristotle: The Revised Oxford Translation*, ed. Jonathan Barnes (Princeton, NJ: Princeton University Press, 1984), 2:1624.

2   Michael J. Loux, *Primary "Ousia": An Essay on Aristotle's Metaphysics Z and H* (Ithaca, NY: Cornell University Press, 1991), 2.

3   Aristotle, *Metaphysics*, 2:1644.

4   Plato, *Sophist*, trans. Nicholas P. White, in *Plato: Complete Works*, ed. John M. Cooper (Indianapolis, IN; Cambridge: Hackett Publishing Company, 1997), 269–70.

5   Plato, *Phaedo*, trans. G. M. A. Grube, in *Plato: Complete Works*, ed. John M. Cooper (Indianapolis, IN; Cambridge: Hackett Publishing Company, 1997), 86.

6   Verity Harte, "Plato's Metaphysics," in *The Oxford Handbook of Plato*, ed. Gail Fine (Oxford: Oxford University Press, 2008), 193–4.

7   Howard Robinson, "Substance," *Stanford Encyclopedia of Philosophy*, accessed February 10, 2015, http://plato.stanford.edu/entries/substance/.

8   Aristotle, *Metaphysics*, 2:1640.

9   Aristotle, *Metaphysics*, 2:1630.

10 Aristotle, *Metaphysics*, 2:1625.

MODULE 4
THE AUTHOR'S CONTRIBUTION

KEY POINTS

- Aristotle criticizes Plato's* Theory of Forms* for considering substance* to be outside of, prior to, and more real than individual bodies. He argues that substance is an immanent* form—that is, a form present in matter.

- Aristotle's theory about substance challenges a common view of his day and raises a viable alternative that would become extremely influential among philosophers for many centuries.

- While Aristotle draws on some of Plato's theoretical assumptions, he provides a genuinely novel take on the pre-existing concepts.

Author's Aims

Aristotle claims in *Metaphysics* that he seeks the knowledge of "causes and principles."[1] In short, he dedicates this work to exploring the questions of the most fundamental ontology,* the study of the nature of being.

Arguably the most important topic he addresses in this work is his theory about substance. Scholars typically explain this theory as a response to Plato. But its importance mainly lies in Aristotle's substantial and well-argued account of substance, which scholars have recognized for centuries as a key contribution to metaphysics.* Although Aristotle may have felt he was simply adding to a well-developed debate, his contribution is an outstanding philosophical achievement in its own right. Aristotle's ideas challenged what had been widely accepted as a strong account of what substance is.

> **❝** All men suppose what is called wisdom to deal with the first causes and the principles of things. This is why, as has been said before, the man of experience is thought to be wiser than the possessors of any perception whatever, the artist wiser than the men of experience, the master-worker than the mechanic, and the theoretical kinds of knowledge to be more of the nature of wisdom than the productive. Clearly then wisdom is knowledge about certain causes and principles. **❞**
>
> Aristotle, *Metaphysics*

As professor of ancient philosophy, Theodore Scaltsas* explains, "Aristotle insists that the substantial form* is not a further component part in a substance, but is of a different ontological type from the component parts. In doing so Aristotle is presenting us with his own theory, but at the same time he is offering a criticism of the Platonic* metaphysics."[2] In addition to showing that Plato's Theory of Forms had problematic aspects as an account of substance, Aristotle aimed to present a very different account of his own. Instead of placing substance in eternal, changeless, incorporeal objects outside of this world (as Plato had), Aristotle argued that substance is a form present in matter—an idea known as the immanence of form. Aristotle supported his argument with both strong analyses and astute observations.

Approach

In his quest to define substance, Aristotle claims to be researching being. He notes that philosophers use the term "being" in a number of different ways, but then goes on to argue that primary being is the substance and then explains that when we talk about substantial being, we distinguish from merely accidental properties* as follows: "when we say of what quality a thing is, we say that it is good or beautiful, but not that it is three cubits long or that it is a man; but when we say what it is, we do not say 'white' or 'hot' or 'three cubits long', but 'man' or 'God.'"[3]

Although the underlying idea is similar to Plato's, Aristotle presents his investigation in a very different manner. Aristotle's thorough, methodical approach to answering very complex questions was unparalleled—both in the ancient world and afterwards."*Metaphysics* … uses Aristotle's most intricate and technical machinery in the service of some of the most demanding and fundamental problems in all of philosophy."[4]

Because Aristotle writes in a technical style and uses many extra concepts and side-investigations to support his search for a strong account of substance, *Metaphysics* remains a notoriously difficult text to read. Aristotle used a unique approach throughout his works. He organized his inquiry based on his idea that in order to investigate something, "one starts with what is familiar to us initially, and moves towards an understanding of first principles that are knowable by nature."[5]

Contribution in Context

Aristotle's account of substance is best understood in the context of his critique of Plato's Theory of Forms. Plato famously theorized about the existence of incorporeal universal* entities—forms—as perfect examples of every existing object. Aristotle criticized Platonic forms, pointing out that the theory is susceptible to various objections, for instance the so-called third man argument.* Aristotle famously argued that if a man becomes a man by partaking* in the form of a man, then the form of a man also requires another form in order to be a form of a man, and so on.[6]

However, Aristotle also used the notion of "form" in his work. He argued that substance is an immanent form, that is, a form present in matter. Aristotle reinterpreted the received idea of the existence of forms and developed it into a distinct theory, "whereas for Plato it seemed vital to assert the existence of the forms apart and by themselves, at the same time as they in some mysterious way 'entered into' the concrete things which were called by their names, for Aristotle they were always in some physical body."[7]

As we can see from his engagement with Plato, Aristotle borrowed concepts from the tradition that already existed however, he also introduced genuinely novel interpretations of these ideas. Although Greek philosophers before him had analyzed the concept of substance, Aristotle's theory made a significant contribution to the debate by raising problems and presenting new interpretations of such concepts as form, which philosophers had not addressed before.

NOTES

1   Aristotle, *Metaphysics*, trans. William David Ross, in *The Complete Works of Aristotle: The Revised Oxford Translation*, ed. Jonathan Barnes (Princeton, NJ: Princeton University Press, 1984), 2:1553–4.

2   Theodore Scaltsas, *Substances and Universals in Aristotle's Metaphysics* (New York: Cornell University Press, 1994), 72.

3   Aristotle, *Metaphysics*, 2:1623.

4   Christopher Shields, *Aristotle* (London: Routledge, 2007), 232–4.

5   Alan Code, "Aristotle's Logic and Metaphysics," in *Routledge History of Philosophy, Volume II: From Aristotle to Augustine*, ed. David Furley (London: Routledge, 1999), 54.

6   Aristotle, *Metaphysics*, 2:1706.

7   W. K. C. Guthrie, *The Greek Philosophers: From Thales to Aristotle* (London: Routledge, 2013), 121.

SECTION 2
IDEAS

MAIN IDEAS

KEY POINTS

- Broadly speaking, the main theme of *Metaphysics* is "being"—specifically as it concerns substance.*

- Substance, according to Aristotle, is the form immanent* in matter. That means, it only exists in matter.

- Aristotle's style makes his complex arguments hard to follow. The coherence of *Metaphysics* as a whole has also been compromised by translation issues.

Key Themes

Broadly speaking, the main theme of Aristotle's *Metaphysics* is being. The author explains that metaphysics* is a science of "being qua being"* (being by virtue of being) and makes a contrast between his inquiry into being and specific sciences such as geometry or physics.[1] In this way, he unites the books of *Metaphysics* by this common theme. As Irish philosopher Terence Irwin* explains, "whatever their literary origins, all these books have a common subject matter, since they all contribute to the universal science that studies the common presuppositions of the other sciences."[2] Specific sciences analyze particular aspects of being, while Aristotle's science, typically referred to as "ontology"* today, concentrates on existence itself. Aristotle discusses the general theme of being in *Metaphysics* by engaging with such themes as substance, change, and the notion of the unmoved mover.*

Aristotle claims that the investigation of being amounts to the investigation of substance.[3] Interestingly, only the central books of *Metaphysics*—Zeta, Eta, and Theta—address substance as the main

> **❝** The formula in which the term itself is not present but its meaning is expressed, this is the formula of the essence of each thing. **❞**
>
> Aristotle, *Metaphysics*.

theme. The contents of Beta, Gamma, Epsilon, Theta, Lambda, Mu, and Nu supplement this discussion in various ways by addressing more or less loosely related topics. The books Delta, which discusses philosophical vocabulary, and Kappa—which contains summaries of Aristotle's ideas from *Metaphysics* and his other work, *Physics*—do not relate to the main discussion of substance in any obvious way.

Exploring the Ideas

We can best understand substances as "ontologically basic entities":[4] that is, the essences of objects. For Aristotle, substances are also principles and causes of being.[5] In *Metaphysics* book Zeta, Aristotle develops a hylomorphic* theory. This theory states that substance is a form present in matter.[6] The formula of this definition is quite nuanced. Rejecting the idea that substance is simply a compound comprising form and matter, Aristotle notes that a compound cannot exist before its constituent parts.[7] The actual substance is a form, but it must be present in matter, because, according to Aristotle, forms are immanent: that is, they do not have independent existence and can only be found in objects. The form of a man, for example, can only be found in a man.

This does not mean, however, that every man has his own peculiar form. A form, according to Aristotle, is an essence, which he defines as "the formula in which the term itself is not present but its meaning is expressed, this is the formula of the essence of each thing."[8] Marc Cohen,* a contemporary philosopher working on Aristotle, suggests that we may best understand this complex definition by considering an essence as equivalent to an object's species.[9] A form present in a particular man gives him essential properties necessary for being a man, but it does not determine his accidental features, for instance the shape of his nose.

Language and Expression

Aristotle's surviving works remain notoriously difficult to read. In *Metaphysics*, he uses highly technical, jargon-filled language and presents his very complex ideas in terse, dense prose. One reason for this may be that he wrote these works as lecture notes for himself, and perhaps for his pupils—"the Aristotelian Corpus, as we have it, largely consists of works that appear to be closely related to Aristotle's lectures."[10] Any student who has tried to make sense of another student's notes can appreciate the challenge Aristotle has left us.

Metaphysics also lacks continuous and coherent narrative—another reason readers find it difficult to understand. We can read most of its books as self-contained and independent treatises. Scholars have not clarified how—or if—Aristotle intended the topics in separate books to complement each other. But at the same time, *Metaphysics* as a whole does have some coherence. We may read it as a collection of different approaches exploring various questions relating to the notion of being. As John Ackrill,* a twentieth-century classicist and philosopher, describes it, Aristotle's philosophy "is not a single, rigid system; nor can the treatises be set out and expounded in a simple chronological order. The real unity in his work is to be found in method, style and intellectual character, and in the pervasiveness of some terminology."[11]

The terminology Aristotle uses in *Metaphysics* has played a role in the development of philosophical vocabulary. "Much of the technical vocabulary of later philosophy is derived from Latin versions of Aristotle's metaphysical terms: for example, 'substance', 'essence', 'quality', 'quantity' and 'category.'"[12] Many, if not all, of the terms we use to describe fundamental reality today were first defined and used in *Metaphysics*. For that reason and many others, the work has an important place in the history of philosophy.

NOTES

1   Aristotle, *Metaphysics*, trans. William David Ross, in *The Complete Works of Aristotle: The Revised Oxford Translation*, ed. Jonathan Barnes (Princeton, NJ: Princeton University Press, 1984), 2:1584.

2   Terence Irwin, "Aristotle," in *The Shorter Routledge Encyclopedia of Philosophy*, ed. Edward Craig (London: Routledge, 2005), 56.

3   Aristotle, *Metaphysics*, 2:1624.

4   Michael J. Loux, *Primary "Ousia": An Essay on Aristotle's Metaphysics Z and H* (Ithaca, NY: Cornell University Press, 1991), 2.

5   Aristotle, *Metaphysics*, 2:1643.

6   Aristotle, *Metaphysics*, 2:1644.

7   Aristotle, *Metaphysics*, 2:1624.

8   Aristotle, *Metaphysics*, 2:1626.

9   S. Marc Cohen, "Substances," in *A Companion to Aristotle*, ed. Georgios Anagnostopoulis (Malden, MA: Wiley-Blackwell, 2009), 203.

10 Terence Irwin and Gail Fine, *Aristotle: Introductory Readings* (Indianapolis, IN: Hackett Publishing Company; 1996), 12.

11 J. L. Ackrill, *Aristotle the Philosopher* (Oxford: Oxford University Press, 1981), 4.

12 David Furley, introduction to *Routledge History of Philosophy, Volume II: From Aristotle to Augustine*, ed. David Furley (London: Routledge, 1999), 4.

MODULE 6
SECONDARY IDEAS

KEY POINTS

- Aristotle introduced the notions of "potentiality"* and "actuality"* to help him offer a solution to Parmenides'* paradox of change. He also introduces the concept of a first cause and of an unmoved mover.*

- These concepts explore different aspects of being, apart from the notion of substance,* but they are very important in their own right.

- Aristotle's ideas on these notions are classic studies of some of the foundational questions of metaphysics.*

Other Ideas

The main idea Aristotle tackles in *Metaphysics* is substance. But concepts such as "potentiality" and "actuality," as well as the nature of God, also contribute to his project of investigating "being qua being."*[1] Aristotle develops his ideas of potentiality and actuality most clearly in his other work, *Physics*. He used these concepts to answer the philosophical problem of change, a question the pre-Socratic* philosopher Parmenides* had raised.

In a notoriously complicated argument, Parmenides maintained that one cannot use the notion of non-being to explain being, since non-being does not exist. Ultimately, this led him to assert that change is impossible, because change involves the generation and destruction of states. "Parmenides rejected pluralism and the reality of any kind of change: for him all was one indivisible, unchanging reality, and any appearances to the contrary were illusions, to be dispelled by reason and revelation."[2]

> **❝ One actuality always precedes another in time right back to the actuality of the eternal prime mover. ❞**
> Aristotle, *Metaphysics*

Because they did not accept the existence of non-being, both Parmenides and Plato* (especially in his middle works) were of the opinion that generation—the act of coming into being from a state of non-being—is impossible. Following that logic, since destruction requires the change from being into non-being, destruction is equally impossible.

In *Metaphysics* book Theta, Aristotle offers an account of change that solves Parmenides' puzzle by distinguishing between being-as-potentiality and being-as-actuality.[3] A child, for instance, exists potentially as an adult and in actuality as a child. As Aristotle saw it, change is not a phenomenon in which non-existence comes into existence, but in which "being potentially" changes into "being actually."

Exploring the Ideas

In *Metaphysics* book Theta, Aristotle uses the concepts of potentiality and actuality to explain the relationship between matter and form in their compound (or amalgamated) existence. According to him, form is actuality and matter is potentiality.[4] For example, an actual block of wood has a potential existence as a statue, because a sculptor can carve it into one. Aristotle held that actuality always precedes potentiality: "one actuality always precedes another in time right back to the actuality of the eternal prime mover."[5] This leads us to the second important idea Aristotle presents in *Metaphysics*: the prime concept of the unmoved mover.

In *Metaphysics* book Alpha, Aristotle states that gods are the first causes and principles.[6] He elaborates on this idea in book Lambda.

First, Aristotle discusses the nature of change as a kind of motion.[7] Then he investigates the types of motion, so he may determine the first cause of all the motion. Aristotle concludes that, "there is, then, something which is always moved with an unceasing motion, which is motion in a circle; and this is plain not in theory only but in fact. Therefore the first heavens must be eternal. There is therefore also something which moves them. And since that which is moved and moves is intermediate, there is a mover which moves without being moved, being eternal, substance, and actuality."[8] This motion is not physical. The unmoved mover causes motion just as desired objects move those who desire them.[9] Aristotle then considers whether there are many unmoved movers or only one.[10] His conclusion about this remains unclear. As philosophy professor Terence Irwin* points out, in *Metaphysics* Lambda Aristotle argues that the movements of every astronomical body originate from a separate unmoved mover, but later he also states that, "the universe is unified by a single first unmoved mover." These two claims remain difficult to reconcile.[11]

Aristotle's original and innovative ideas about change and the unmoved mover solved known philosophical problems in his time. They also stand as substantial contributions to philosophical debates right to the present day.

Overlooked

Aristotle's *Metaphysics* covers many themes and contains multiple arguments. In part, this accounts for its popularity through the ages. Anyone interested in metaphysics and its history will seek out and analyze *Metaphysics*. In thousands of years of analysis, scholars have not overlooked much about this work. Its central topics—substance, change, essence, God—and Aristotle's smaller observations and inferences, such as the ideas that the object can be more than the sum of its parts,[12] have been studied meticulously.

At the same time, there is still room to discover and reinterpret certain topics Aristotle covers in *Metaphysics*. American philosopher Jonathan Beere's* book *Doing and Being: An Interpretation of Aristotle's Metaphysics Theta*[13] examines Aristotle's use of the terms *energeia* and *dunamis* in *Metaphysics*. A simple explanation is that *energeia* is actuality and *dunamis* means potentiality but Aristotle used these terms in very complicated ways and it is difficult to give their precise theoretical definitions. By means of careful analysis of the ways in which Aristotle uses these terms and the ways in which he describes them theoretically, Beere resolves major arguments from *Metaphysics* Theta.

NOTES

1 Aristotle, *Metaphysics*, trans. William David Ross, in *The Complete Works of Aristotle: The Revised Oxford Translation*, ed. Jonathan Barnes (Princeton, NJ: Princeton University Press, 1984), 2:1584.

2 Nick Huggett, "Zeno's Paradoxes," *Stanford Encyclopedia of Philosophy*, accessed February 11, 2015, http://plato.stanford.edu/entries/paradox-zeno/.

3 Aristotle, *Metaphysics*, 2:1656–7.

4 Aristotle, *Metaphysics*, 2:1659.

5 Aristotle, *Metaphysics*, 2:1659.

6 Aristotle, *Metaphysics*, 2:1555.

7 Aristotle, *Metaphysics*, 2:1690.

8 Aristotle, Metaphysics, 2:1694.

9 Aristotle, *Metaphysics*, 2:1694.

10 Aristotle, Metaphysics, 2:1697–8.

11 Terence Irwin, "Aristotle," in *The Shorter Routledge Encyclopedia of Philosophy*, ed. Edward Craig (London: Routledge, 2005), 59.

12 Aristotle, *Metaphysics*, 2:1650.

13 Jonathan Beere, *Doing and Being: An Interpretation of Aristotle's Metaphysics Theta* (Oxford: Oxford University Press, 2009).

MODULE 7
ACHIEVEMENT

KEY POINTS

- Aristotle's main achievement in *Metaphysics* is to present a number of thorough, rigorous studies on the theme of being.
- Aristotle's approach and method contributed to the quality and lasting reputation of the work.
- His theory about substance* prevailed for nearly two thousand years, up until the early modern period* (1450–1750).

Assessing the Argument

In composing *Metaphysics,* Aristotle mainly aimed to explore the most fundamental ontological* questions, that is the "causes and principles" of being.[1] But he died before completing *Metaphysics* and left the work somewhat disjointed and lacking in a clear structure. The books Beta, Gamma, Epsilon, Zeta, Eta, and Theta clearly explore ontological topics, especially the issue of existence. The rest of the books treat topics that are not obvious parts of the main discussion.

Aristotle did not decide on the order of the books as we read them today. About three centuries after his death, the Roman editor Andronicus* collected Aristotle's treatises on related topics and published them under the title of *Metaphysics*. For this reason, we cannot know what Aristotle intended his finished account to achieve. Most likely, he wanted to produce a study of the fundamental nature of everything that exists, and in doing so, to introduce and develop a thorough understanding of philosophy's most fundamental questions, such as what a substance is, how to explain change, and how to understand first causes.

❝ When Aristotle articulated the central question of the group of writings we know as his *Metaphysics*, he said it was a question that would never cease to raise itself. He was right. He also regarded his own contributions to the handling of that question as belonging to the final phase of responding to it. I think he was right about that too. The *Metaphysics* is one of the most helpful books there is for contending with a question the asking of which is one of the things that makes us human. ❞

Joe Sachs, "Aristotle: Metaphysics"

The ideas in *Metaphysics* do have a certain conceptual unity. All the books contain discussions relating to metaphysics.* While Aristotle does not always link the arguments to one another explicitly, *Metaphysics* remains a compelling collection of studies on the nature of being.

To the extent that Aristotle set out to provide an account of being, his work remains very successful. He not only engaged with some of the most difficult metaphysical questions, he also proposed possible answers. His strong, compelling ontological account rivals the Platonic* metaphysics of his day and has been recognized as an important contribution to metaphysics for centuries. Aristotle translator Joe Sachs notes, "when Aristotle articulated the central question of the group of writings we know as his *Metaphysics*, he said it was a question that would never cease to raise itself. He was right. He also regarded his own contributions to the handling of that question as belonging to the final phase of responding to it. I think he was right about that too. The *Metaphysics* is one of the most helpful books there is for contending with a question the asking of which is one of the things that makes us human."[2]

Achievement in Context

In his lifetime and in ours, *Metaphysics* has remained popular, as have Aristotle's other works. Some scholars used to argue that after the death of his close followers, Aristotle's works became virtually forgotten until they were published in the Roman* period. Today scholars generally agree that Aristotle's ideas were known throughout the Hellenistic period*—the three centuries between the death of Alexander the Great* and the rise of the ancient Roman Empire.[3]

Metaphysics also exerted a great influence on early Islamic* philosophers. Important thinkers, such as the early twelfth-century legal scholar and philosopher Averroes (Ibn Rushd),* wrote commentaries on Aristotle's work and used his concepts in their own works. While Aristotle and other ancient philosophers were hardly known in the early Middle Ages* (beginning in the twelfth century C.E.), Aristotle's works gradually became more widely available in Europe. This re-emergence of Aristotle's writings set off great interest in his thought among European thinkers.

The main topic of Aristotle's *Metaphysics*—substance—has remained a classic metaphysical notion and a central concern of metaphysics since the time he first discussed it. Philosophers in the ancient world, and those in the Middle Ages, considered *Metaphysics* a work of great importance. Aristotle's account of substance as a form present in matter rivaled the earlier Platonic idea that substances must be incorporeal,* timeless forms existing outside the tangible world. Ancient and medieval* metaphysicians debated the merits of Plato's* or Aristotle's accounts of substance and used them as reference points to construct their own accounts. This is why the text maintained a central role in philosophical debates for many centuries.

Limitations

One might describe *Metaphysics* as the product of its time, because it concerns itself with topics that were most relevant to philosophers in the Classical period.* But nonetheless, it remained an important work for many centuries after Aristotle wrote it.

In the modern period, however, a critique issued by the eighteenth-century Scottish philosopher David Hume* challenged the work's relevance. Hume argued that because Aristotle had not based his notion of substance on any evidence, philosophers should discard it. Instead, Hume proposed a so-called bundle theory:* essences of objects are nothing but the sum of all their properties.[4] Aristotle believed that particular properties of a man, such as a snub nose or height, do not explain what it is to be a man. However, Hume argued the opposite. This criticism did not erase Aristotle from philosophical debate completely, but it did substantially diminish his influence. More importantly, the focus of philosophical discussions began to shift. With Hume's rejection of the very notion of substance, philosophers started investigating alternative ways of accounting for what the essence of being is. Eventually, scholars began to class Aristotle's thought under "history of philosophy." *Metaphysics* and his other works no longer appeared to be at the cutting edge of the discipline.

NOTES

1 Aristotle, *Metaphysics*, trans. William David Ross, in *The Complete Works of Aristotle: The Revised Oxford Translation*, ed. Jonathan Barnes (Princeton, NJ: Princeton University Press, 1984), 2:1553.

2 Joe Sachs, "Aristotle: Metaphysics," Internet Encyclopedia of Philosophy, accessed February 10, 2015, http://www.iep.utm.edu/aris-met/.

3 Jonathan Barnes, "Life and work," in *The Cambridge Companion to Aristotle*, ed. Jonathan Barnes (Cambridge: Cambridge University Press, 1995), 10–11.

4 See, for instance, David Hume, *Treatise* 1.4.6.3.

MODULE 8
PLACE IN THE AUTHOR'S WORK

KEY POINTS

- Aristotle wrote a huge number of treatises on a wide variety of topics.

- He also looks into the central topics of *Metaphysics* in his books *Categories* and *Physics*.

- *Metaphysics* remains one of Aristotle's best-known and most important works.

Positioning

When did Aristotle compose *Metaphysics*? Scholars have debated this question extensively. Until the twentieth century, academics viewed Aristotle's works as a consistent and finished whole—treating the entire Aristotelian corpus as the product of a mature thinker. Over the last 100 years, however, scholars have challenged this view and it is now generally rejected. Thomas Case,* an early twentieth-century philosopher who worked on Aristotle, argued that it would have taken Aristotle many years to produce the sheer volume of works he authored. So it remains unlikely he composed them all at the end of his life. Instead, Case argues that Aristotle kept his works as manuscripts and worked on them continuously throughout his career.[1]

The lack of unity among the books of *Metaphysics* also supports this interpretation. The variety of topics and their lack of coherent connections clearly indicates that Aristotle did not produce *Metaphysics* in a conventional manner—writing the entire work at once. So it may well have been composed over a longer time period. Jonathan Barnes,* a well-known Aristotelian scholar, has pointed out that ancient commentaries on *Metaphysics* imply that Aristotle died before

> ❝ A prodigious researcher and writer, Aristotle left a great body of work, perhaps numbering as many as two-hundred treatises, from which approximately thirty-one survive. ❞
>
> Christopher Shields, "Aristotle" in *Stanford Encyclopedia of Philosophy*

editing the work properly, leaving it in an incoherent state.[2] Overall, scholars tend to agree that *Metaphysics* must have been a product of continuous work throughout Aristotle's lifetime, and that he may indeed have left it unfinished when he died.

The central theme developed in *Metaphysics*, the idea of substance,* can also be found in another of Aristotle's works, *Categories*. Although there is no clear evidence suggesting that Aristotle wrote *Categories* before *Metaphysics*, "it is easier to understand the relation of the doctrine of substance in the *Categories* … to the doctrine and argument of *Metaphysics* 7 if we supposed that *Metaphysics* 7 is later."[3] Students often read *Categories* before *Metaphysics* as an introduction to the notion of substance, because it presents some simpler ideas. For instance, in *Categories*, Aristotle defines substance as that which is capable of receiving contraries while being numerically singular.[4] To help readers understand this idea, Aristotle provided an example: because a color cannot be black and white while remaining the same color, color is not substance. But a man can be pale and become tanned while remaining the same man. So being a man is a substance. This idea shows that we ought to understand substances as explanations of what it is like to be, for instance, a man. In *Categories,* Aristotle points out that if we wish to know what the essence of being a man is, we cannot simply look at any properties that a man might have. A man can be pale or old or an Athenian citizen, but being pale, old, and an Athenian citizen do not explain what it is to be a man. For this reason, Aristotle suggests that we need to determine what the substance of man is by investigating what aspects of a man persist through all changes.

Integration

"A prodigious researcher and writer, Aristotle left a great body of work, perhaps numbering as many as two-hundred treatises, from which approximately thirty-one survive."[5] Although we have only a relatively small portion of Aristotle's works, those surviving texts cover a wide range of topics, from metaphysics* to politics. Even among ancient philosophers who often produced large numbers of wide-ranging treatises, Aristotle's achievement is outstanding.

The range of Aristotle's works can also be useful in helping understand some of his more complex ideas. Scholars and philosophers commonly read and cross-reference works such as *Physics, Categories,* (and sometimes even *On the Soul*), and *Metaphysics.* "Some of the basic concepts of the *Categories* and *Physics*—including substance, particular, universal,* form, matter, cause and potentiality—are discussed more fully in the *Metaphysics*."[6] When looking to understand the ideas Aristotle presents in *Metaphysics,* we do well to consider the arguments and ideas in his other works that address the same or similar issues. But it is also possible to read different works together to find out what Aristotle's overall stance was on some general question. For instance, if we want to consider what Aristotle thought about the nature of human beings, we would find it useful to read not only *Metaphysics* or *On the Soul,* but also *Nicomachean Ethics* and *Politics.*

Significance

While Aristotle wrote many groundbreaking treatises in various areas of philosophy, *Metaphysics* is still one of his most important works. Aristotle's innovative way of thinking has made his body of work vastly influential to later philosophers. But even if he had written nothing but *Metaphysics,* Aristotle would have had a great impact in the history of philosophy. First adopted and disseminated by Aristotle's followers, the Peripatetics,* the ideas in *Metaphysics* have resounded through the centuries. Many different people have studied them, from ancient Greek and Roman* philosophers to medieval* thinkers, Islamic* intellectuals, and modern philosophers.

However, because of developments in the discipline of philosophy, Aristotle's influence began to wane during the early modern* period in the mid-fifteenth century. Philosophers largely rejected the topic of substance. This was not only because new theories and ideas had emerged, but also because the philosophical focus started shifting to different topics. This, in turn, decreased Aristotle's relevance. Yet this does not diminish his overall achievement. Even if philosophers no longer accept some of Aristotle's concepts and arguments, he remains one of the most important thinkers in the history of philosophy. Scholars still discuss the historical *and* philosophical importance of certain aspects of his thought. *Categories*, *Physics*, and especially *Metaphysics* earned Aristotle acclaim as one of the most important metaphysicians in Western philosophy.

NOTES

1 Thomas Case, "Aristotle," in *Aristotle's Philosophical Development: Problems and Prospects*, ed. William Wians (Lanham, MD: Rowman & Littlefield, 1996), 13.

2 Jonathan Barnes, "Roman Aristotle," in *Philosophia Togata II, Plato and Aristotle at Rome*, ed. Jonathan Barnes and Miriam Griffin (Oxford: Clarendon Press, 1997), 61–2.

3 Terence Irwin, "Aristotle," in *The Shorter Routledge Encyclopedia of Philosophy*, ed. Edward Craig (London: Routledge, 2005), 51.

4 Aristotle, *Categories*, trans. John L. Ackrill, in *The Complete Works of Aristotle: The Revised Oxford Translation*, ed. Jonathan Barnes (Princeton, NJ: Princeton University Press, 1984), 1:7.

5 Christopher Shields, "Aristotle," *Stanford Encyclopedia of Philosophy*, accessed February 10, 2015, http://plato.stanford.edu/entries/aristotle/.

6 Irwin, "Aristotle," 56.

SECTION 3
IMPACT

MODULE 9
THE FIRST RESPONSES

KEY POINTS

- Plotinus* criticized Aristotle's views by arguing that failing to include accidental properties* in the notion of substance* leaves one unable to distinguish between individual substances.

- Commentators such as Alexander of Aphrodisias* advocated Aristotle's views against the views of such rival schools as Stoicism.*

- Overall, Aristotle's ideas were very well received and inspired many philosophers to develop their own ideas.

Criticism

In *Metaphysics,* Aristotle criticizes the existing philosophical tradition. But, surprisingly, the author received little explicit criticism himself. In Aristotle's most immediate circle, his own followers—known as the Peripatetics*—appear to have been more interested in preserving his works than debating them. Interestingly, this trend continued even after Aristotle's original Lyceum* school disbanded. In later antiquity,* Aristotle's works became a popular source for commentators such as Alexander of Aphrodisias, who explained Aristotle's views and criticized rival philosophical accounts.

Even the Neoplatonists,* who identified themselves with Plato's* thought, did not reject Aristotle's metaphysics* entirely. Often they studied it alongside Plato's work. Ilsetraut Hadot,* a present-day scholar working on ancient philosophy, has argued that the Neoplatonic philosophers found that Plato's and Aristotle's works could be studied side by side. Yet, "Plato's philosophy, by contrast with

❝ Plato's philosophy, by contrast with Aristotle's, is considered the more elevated, the more theological, the more inspired. It is likewise clear that the *Metaphysics* can only be a half-stage between the studies of natural principles and natural causes, and the true theology developed by Plato in his *Parmenides*. Aristotle's thought is not, by nature, sufficiently 'transcendent'. ❞

Ilsetraut Hadot, "The Role of the Commentaries on Aristotle in the Teaching of Philosophy according to the Prefaces of the Neoplatonic Commentaries on the Categories"

Aristotle's, is considered the more elevated, the more theological, the more inspired. It is likewise clear that the *Metaphysics* can only be a half-stage between the studies of natural principles and natural causes, and the true theology developed by Plato in his *Parmenides*. Aristotle's thought is not, by nature, sufficiently 'transcendent'."[1]

One exception to this trend stands out: Plotinus's critique of Aristotle's idea of substance in his seminal work *Enneads*. Plotinus employs various arguments to reject Aristotle's idea that substance is immanent* form, present in matter. He also defends a Platonic* notion of form as existing beyond the sensible world, the world we can see and feel. Lloyd Gerson,* a noted expert on ancient philosophy, has suggested that Plotinus identified a problem with Aristotle's account of substance when he argued that Aristotle could not reasonably maintain that substances are immanent in an object. If we assume that accidental properties* (such as having a snub nose, for example) are not part of the essence, then nothing in the essence requires it to belong to a particular object. For instance, such a notion of essence does not distinguish between Plato and Socrates.* In Plotinus's view, this renders Aristotle's account of substance unjustifiable.[2]

Responses

Aristotle did not have a chance to respond to contemporary critiques of *Metaphysics*, because the evidence that exists suggests that most appeared after his death. During his lifetime, Aristotle most probably engaged in many critical debates. He may even have altered his views in response to criticisms, but no evidence of this survives. This lack of evidence makes it impossible to know with absolute certainty how Aristotle might have been criticized and what effect such criticism may have had on him.

After Aristotle's death, his followers, commonly called the Peripatetics, took up the task of promoting Aristotle's thought and responding to criticism. Peripatetic commentators such as Alexander of Aphrodisias, who wrote a commentary on *Metaphysics*, advocated Aristotle's ideas against those of other philosophical schools such as the Stoics. Aristotle's supporters also responded to those who explored the differences between Platonic and Aristotelian thought.

However, these commentators were not necessarily responding to criticism of Aristotle. They were merely addressing alternative theories as other groups raised them. What remains of Stoic thinking, for instance, does not criticize or even mention Aristotle explicitly. But commentaries defending Aristotle against either implicit or perceived criticism allowed his thought to remain relevant long after it was published.

Conflict and Consensus

The ideas Aristotle presented in *Metaphysics* have been widely read, discussed, and debated since antiquity. Philosophers considered Platonism* the main rival for the philosophy Aristotle set out in the work. That said, even thinkers with Platonic or other philosophical leanings appreciated *Metaphysics*. The critical debate with the Platonists did not necessarily affect the work's reception, either in Aristotle's time or afterwards. We can best understand the rivalry between Platonism and Aristotelianism as an ongoing discussion of the advantages and shortcomings of both these schools of thought. Nobody on either side of the debate denied either theory completely.

Many important thinkers have mounted interesting defenses of Aristotle-inspired metaphysics. According to the Canadian philosopher Claude Panaccio,* the thirteenth-century cleric Thomas Aquinas* "rejected Platonism for having wrongly supposed that universals* have to exist in a separate manner in the extra-mental world to be correctly isolated by the mind … Even though universals in the strict sense exist only in the mind for him, they nevertheless have an external foundation within the singular things: human nature is somehow in each singular human being."[3]

As Panaccio's modern analysis makes clear, Aristotelian views were talked about and discussed for many centuries after Aristotle's death. And a lively debate still rages between thinkers who sympathize with Aristotle's ideas and those who favor Platonic or Neoplatonic theories. Although some thinkers claimed to have definitively refuted Aristotle's metaphysical account, later philosophers revived and defended it, allowing it to inspire new thought.

NOTES

1   Ilsetraut Hadot, "The Role of the Commentaries on Aristotle in the Teaching of Philosophy according to the Prefaces of the Neoplatonic Commentaries on the Categories," *Oxford Studies of Ancient Philosophy* supp. vol. (1991): 184.

2   Lloyd Gerson, *Plotinus* (London and New York: Routledge, 1994), 93–6.

3   Claude Panaccio, "Medieval Metaphysics 1: The Problem of Universals," in *The Routledge Companion to Metaphysics*, ed. Robin Le Poidevin et al. (London and New York: Routledge, 2009), 52.

MODULE 10
THE EVOLVING DEBATE

KEY POINTS

- Aristotle's *Metaphysics* played an important role in the works of later thinkers such as Thomas Aquinas* and Avicenna (Ibn Sīnā).*

- Aristotle's followers, the Peripatetics,* formed a school of thought, but it did not last beyond the Hellenistic period.*

- *Metaphysics* played an important role in the development of the discipline that took its name from the book. Aristotle's work introduced new ideas and arguments that became central to the field and inspired various philosophers to go on to produce their own analyses of its topics.

Uses and Problems

Aristotle's *Metaphysics* greatly influenced the evolution of philosophy in general, and in particular of the discipline that came to be called "metaphysics."* Aristotle's critique of Plato's* idea that substances* are incorporeal* forms played an especially important role in the development of metaphysics.

For later philosophers, such as Neoplatonists* or medieval* metaphysicians, the Platonic* and Aristotelian accounts of substance represented a great dilemma. While Plato theorized that incorporeal, eternal forms exist as substances, Aristotle's account suggests that substances only exist as immanent* forms—that is, as forms existing in matter. Philosophers saw both accounts as important, yet they remained incompatible. This incompatibility led to a great debate among thinkers. Some chose one of the views and defended it against the other. Others chose to sidestep the problem and develop an

> ❝ Platonism and Aristotelianism were to become the dominant philosophies of the Western tradition from the second century A.D. at least until the end of the Renaissance, and the legacy of both remains central to Western philosophy today. ❞
>
> David Sedley, from "Ancient Philosophy" in *Routledge Encyclopedia of Philosophy*

account that approached the idea of being in an entirely different manner. As British philosopher David Sedley* notes: "Platonism* and Aristotelianism were to become the dominant philosophies of the Western tradition from the second century A.D. at least until the end of the Renaissance,* and the legacy of both remains central to Western philosophy today."[1]

Aristotle's thought was also very important for the Islamic* philosophical tradition. His metaphysics influenced such prominent thinkers as the tenth-century C.E. Persian physician Ibn Sīnā (or, in Latinate form, Avicenna). Together with other Islamic philosophers, Ibn Sīnā read *Metaphysics* as an important foundational work in ontology,* and also used Aristotelian concepts, such as substance, to develop his own original ideas. Ibn Sīnā wrote three encyclopedias. The first of these, *al-Shifa' (The Cure)*, is "a work modelled on the corpus of the philosopher, namely, Aristotle, that covers the natural sciences, logic, mathematics, metaphysics and theology."[2]

Philosophers in medieval Europe also considered *Metaphysics* a foundational text and debated the differences between Platonism and Aristotelianism and their respective views on the nature of substance. Medieval metaphysicians often adopted one of the two accounts and presented their own notions based on it. Possibly the most famous medieval philosopher influenced by Aristotle was the thirteenth-century Italian cleric Thomas Aquinas: "every part of Aquinas' philosophy is imbued with metaphysical principles, many of which are recognizably Aristotelian. Consequently, concepts such as potentiality and actuality,* matter and form, substance, essence …—all of which are fundamental in Aquinas' metaphysics—should be considered in their original Aristotelian context."[3]

Aristotle's works—including *Metaphysics*—continue to influence philosophers today, especially those who defend a view that substances or essential properties exist that are distinct from merely accidental properties.*

Schools of Thought

Aristotle's own philosophical school, the Lyceum,* lasted only a short time. His works, including *Metaphysics*, were at first read only in the school he founded. But around three centuries later, a Roman editor, Andronicus,* collected and published them. In the intervening period Aristotle received less attention than during his lifetime, but Andronicus's publication revived interest in his thought.

After Aristotle died in 322 B.C.E., his followers—the Peripatetics—kept the Lyceum going. But they saw their most important work as preserving Aristotle's legacy and working in the tradition of his thought. As the well-known Aristotelian scholar Robert Sharples* notes, the early Peripatetics were most interested in gathering information in various fields of study and resolving theoretical difficulties. The school became less popular during the Hellenistic period, but continued until the Romans conquered Athens* in the first century B.C.E.

The second wave of interest in Aristotelian thought happened about 300 years later, during the Roman period,* possibly when Andronicus published Aristotle's works. The increasing number of commentaries on his works at this time demonstrates Aristotle's hold on a new generation of philosophers. Among those whose work survives, the best-known commentator is Alexander of Aphrodisias,* who wrote about *Metaphysics* in particular.

After antiquity,* the period of Western civilization before the Middle Ages,* philosophers discussed Aristotle's ideas less frequently in the philosophical context in which he had presented them. Instead, thinkers applied the concepts that he introduced to a variety of philosophical issues. We cannot call these later thinkers Aristotle's "followers," but his work clearly influenced them as they developed their own views. For instance, medieval logicians (people studying or skilled in logic) applied Aristotle's concepts of matter and form to explain syllogisms, the logical process where two general statements lead to a more particular statement.[4]

Irish philosopher Terence Irwin* suggests, "modern historical study of Aristotle begins in the nineteenth century. It has led to philosophical reassessment, and his works have once again become a source of philosophical insight and argument. Many of the themes of Aristotelian philosophy—the nature of substance, the relation of form to matter … —have reappeared as issues in philosophical debates, and Aristotle's contribution to these debates has influenced the course of philosophical discussion."[5]

In Current Scholarship

Overall, Aristotle's *Metaphysics* enjoys great popularity among philosophers, historians of philosophy, and intellectuals today. Contemporary thinkers often use the ideas presented in *Metaphysics* to inspire their own theories. But scholars still approach *Metaphysics* exegetically* as well—using critical analysis and careful study to work out its original meaning. Whatever their purpose in reading *Metaphysics*, the work remains extremely important, not only for the development of the discipline it gave its name to, but also as a philosophical work in its own right.

In the various guides to *Metaphysics*, such as British scholar Jonathan Barnes's* *Cambridge Companion to Aristotle*[6] and John Ackrill's* *Aristotle the Philosopher*[7] or Michael Loux's *Primary "Ousia":*

An Essay on Aristotle's Metaphysics Z and H,[8] scholars look for the most accurate interpretation of the ideas found in *Metaphysics*, attempting to uncover Aristotle's original meaning. This approach involves not only interpreting ideas, but also investigating the circumstances surrounding how the text was written. For instance, scholars generally agree that Aristotle wrote the books of *Metaphysics* himself; but did Aristotle put them into their existing order or was that done by later editors? This question is still open to debate. But historically minded interpreters such as Barnes concern themselves primarily with the question of how *Metaphysics* itself ought to be understood.

NOTES

1   David Sedley, "Ancient Philosophy," in *The Shorter Routledge Encyclopedia of Philosophy*, ed. Edward Craig (London: Routledge, 2005), 17.

2   Sajjad Rizvi, "Avicenna (Ibn Sīnā)," Internet Encyclopedia of Philosophy, accessed February 11, 2015, http://www.iep.utm.edu/avicenna/.

3   Norman Kretzmann and Eleonore Stump, "Thomas Aquinas," in *The Shorter Routledge Encyclopedia of Philosophy*, ed. Edward Craig (London: Routledge, 2005), 36.

4   Paul Thom, "Logical Form," in *The Handbook of Medieval Philosophy*, ed. John Marenbon (Oxford: Oxford University Press, 2013), 273.

5   Terence Irwin, "Aristotle," in *The Shorter Routledge Encyclopedia of Philosophy*, ed. Edward Craig (London: Routledge, 2005), 67.

6   Jonathan Barnes, ed., *The Cambridge Companion to Aristotle* (Cambridge: Cambridge University Press, 1995).

7   J. L. Ackrill, *Aristotle the Philosopher* (Oxford: Oxford University Press, 1981).

8   Michael Loux, *Primary "Ousia": An Essay on Aristotle's Metaphysics Z and H* (Ithaca, NY: Cornell University Press, 1991).

MODULE 11
IMPACT AND INFLUENCE TODAY

KEY POINTS

- Today *Metaphysics* is considered a classic in the field of metaphysics.*

- The philosophical position called essentialism* derives from Aristotle's work, and it has been both criticized and defended over the last few hundred years.

- A revival of interest in metaphysics during the latter half of the twentieth century has led to more contemporary philosophers looking to Aristotle for ideas and inspiration.

Position

Widely recognized as one of the most important works in the history of philosophy—especially the discipline that took its name from the book—Aristotle's *Metaphysics* remains important today, almost two thousand years after he wrote it.

Contemporary philosophers still find some of Aristotle's arguments substantial enough to use as inspiration. In some cases, Aristotle's ideas even serve as a platform for developing new ideas. The combination of these two factors makes Aristotle "… among the greatest philosophers of all time. Judged solely in terms of his philosophical influence, only Plato is his peer: Aristotle's works shaped centuries of philosophy from Late Antiquity through the Renaissance,* and even today continue to be studied with keen, non-antiquarian interest."[1]

As for Aristotle's influence in contemporary debates, philosophers fall into two camps. On the one hand, philosophers no longer consider some of the central topics that Aristotle looks at in *Metaphysics*, such as substance,* to be significant. But there was a revival of interest in

> **❝** Aristotle numbers among the greatest philosophers of all time. Judged solely in terms of his philosophical influence, only Plato is his peer: Aristotle's works shaped centuries of philosophy from Late Antiquity through the Renaissance, and even today continue to be studied with keen, non-antiquarian interest … His extant writings span a wide range of disciplines, from logic, metaphysics and philosophy of mind, through ethics … In all these areas, Aristotle's theories have provided illumination, met with resistance, sparked debate, and generally stimulated the sustained interest of an abiding readership. **❞**
>
> Christopher Shields, "Aristotle" in *Stanford Encyclopedia of Philosophy*.

metaphysics in the second half of the twentieth century. As a result, contemporary metaphysicians turn to Aristotle's ideas as inspiration and as a point of reference. John Ackrill,* a classicist and philosopher, notes that the "topics of very many books and articles published since then are straight out of Aristotle. Things and qualities, matter and change, count-nouns and mass-words, subject and predicate: such topics are at the centre of Aristotle's investigation and his approach to them has the same linguistic emphasis and sensitivity as that of recent metaphysicians."[2]

Interaction

Ideas found in Aristotle's *Metaphysics* still challenge and influence contemporary philosophical debates. But today's philosophers rarely use Aristotle's arguments directly. The way he discussed philosophical issues differs starkly from the way modern philosophers ask questions. Some of the concepts, theoretical assumptions, and even philosophical methods popular today cannot be found in Aristotle. Yet philosophers still draw useful and inspiring content from works like *Metaphysics* by approaching Aristotle in a loose and interpretative way. For instance, Aristotle's notion of the difference between substantial and accidental properties* inspired the modern theory of essentialism, which holds that every entity has certain core attributes that constitute its identity and function.

Essentialism challenges such popular ideas as bundle theory.* This theory, introduced by Scottish Enlightenment* philosopher David Hume* in the eighteenth century, states that objects are just sums of their properties and no additional entities—such as substances or essential properties—are involved in forming an identity of an object.[3] The recent revival of interest in essentialism and Aristotle's ideas about substances shows that although bundle theory has been popular for several centuries, philosophers can challenge it by reinterpreting ancient ideas (like those of Aristotle) to fit the context of contemporary metaphysics.

The Continuing Debate

In 1973 the American bioethicist Baruch Brody* published an article entitled "Why Settle for Anything Less than Good Old-Fashioned Aristotelian essentialism?" Brody defended a view that there is a distinction between accidental and essential properties that resembles Aristotle's idea of substance. According to Brody, Aristotle correctly noted that some properties are essential in a sense that they constitute what it means to be, for instance, a man. Brody uses the tools of contemporary analytic philosophy* to show the advantages of the notion of essential properties, loosely derived from Aristotle's *Metaphysics*. Similarly, American philosophers Joshua Hoffman* and Gary Rosenkrantz* have also defended the notion of substance. They start by analyzing Aristotle's concept of substance and ultimately reject it for being insufficiently detailed for contemporary metaphysics; but Aristotle's ideas clearly inspired their own account.[4]

The advocates of essentialism remain a minority, yet philosophers recognize they have made important contributions to metaphysical debates about the nature and identity of properties. By interpreting *Metaphysics* broadly, modern philosophers have been able to use its ideas in contemporary thought. In this way *Metaphysics* remains significant not only as a work that helped to shape the field of metaphysics, but also as a source of ideas considered interesting and persuasive even today.

NOTES

1 Christopher Shields, "Aristotle," *Stanford Encyclopedia of Philosophy*, accessed February 10, 2015, http://plato.stanford.edu/entries/aristotle/.

2 J. L. Ackrill, *Aristotle the Philosopher* (Oxford: Oxford University Press, 1981), 8.

3 See, for instance, David Hume, *Treatise* 1.4.6.3.

4 Joshua Hoffman and Gary S. Rosenkrantz, *Substance: Its Nature and Existence* (London and New York: Routledge, 1997).

MODULE 12
WHERE NEXT?

KEY POINTS

- *Metaphysics* is very likely to remain a key work in the field.

- It will be studied both for its historic and its philosophical value.

- Few other works have had such a profound influence on the development of the field of metaphysics* specifically, and philosophical debate more generally.

Potential

Aristotle's *Metaphysics* has played a significant role in philosophical discussions ever since it was produced. It is likely to remain a very important work for philosophers and other thinkers.

Metaphysics was an essential influence in the development of this branch of philosophy in the ancient world, as well as in medieval* Western and Islamic* philosophy. Most, if not all, philosophers from these traditions learned from and were inspired by Aristotle's work. As British philosopher Jonathan Barnes* put it, "an account of Aristotle's intellectual afterlife would be little less than a history of European thought."[1]

Today we seem to be in the midst of a more general revival of interest in Aristotelian philosophy. American philosopher Edward Feser* comments that, "while it would certainly be an overstatement to say that a full-scale revival of Aristotelianism is currently underway, it does seem that some of the various strands of thought alluded to are at least beginning to coalesce into something like a self-conscious movement."[2]

Metaphysics has remained at the center of scholarly attention because of its philosophical content. Today, the text has a somewhat

> **❝** An account of Aristotle's intellectual afterlife would be little less than a history of European thought. **❞**
> Jonathan Barnes, *A Very Short Introduction to Aristotle*

more limited influence than in previous generations. Contemporary philosophers generally consider Aristotle's main topic—substance*—a somewhat outdated concept.

Because contemporary concerns diverge from ancient ones, thinkers inspired by Aristotle's metaphysical doctrines today do not typically use his exact arguments. Instead, they use concepts that Aristotle introduced, such as the notion of essence, being, hylomorphism,* or potentiality and actuality.* Reinterpreting these concepts, modern philosophers incorporate them into discussions of contemporary issues. Since Aristotle's *Metaphysics* is a large and complex work, future philosophers are likely to continue to find inspiration in its pages.

Future Directions

Aristotle's *Metaphysics* continues to be essential reading for philosophers, historians of philosophy, and intellectuals. Believing the work occupies an important place not only in the development of metaphysics, but as a philosophical work in its own right, thinkers interested in *Metaphysics* for exegetical* reasons attempt to interpret the text in a way that allows them to uncover Aristotle's original meaning. This approach involves not only interpreting his ideas, but also investigating the circumstances surrounding the text's composition. Scholars generally agree that Aristotle himself wrote the books of *Metaphysics* but they disagree on whether Aristotle or later editors put them into their existing order.

In contrast, historically minded interpreters generally focus on the question of how we should understand *Metaphysics*. The best examples of this approach can be found in various studies and commentaries such as scholar Jonathan Beere's* *Doing and Being: An Interpretation of Aristotle's Metaphysics Theta*[3] or philosopher David Bostock's* translation and commentary on *Metaphysics* books Zeta and Eta.[4]

Other contemporary thinkers use the ideas presented in *Metaphysics* as inspiration for their own theories. Typically less concerned with Aristotle's original meaning, these scholars evaluate and debate the philosophy of Aristotle's ideas. Recently, for example, the American philosophers Joshua Hoffman* and Gary Rosenkrantz* argued that the notion of a substance—and especially the Aristotelian distinction between substance and accidental properties*—is not only philosophically interesting, but in their view it is, in fact, preferable to metaphysical accounts that reject the existence of substances.[5] After discussing Aristotle's ideas, Hoffman and Rosenkrantz introduced their own ideas that were influenced by Aristotle's account of substance.

Contemporary Finnish philosopher Tuomas Tahko* also has a continuing interest in Aristotle's *Metaphysics*. In his most recent work, he argued that accepting the Aristotelian notion of metaphysics as "the first philosophy" is useful when thinking about the scope of contemporary metaphysics.[6]

These modern works show that two millennia after its composition, *Metaphysics* continues to be of great importance for philosophy.

Summary

Aristotle's *Metaphysics* has been central to the development of philosophical ideas for close to two thousand years. Scholars today read and discuss this seminal work not only because it plays a very important role in the history of philosophy, but also because the ideas it presents continue to crop up in philosophical debates. Even contemporary thinkers find inspiration in Aristotle's ancient concepts and arguments.

Aristotle's *Metaphysics* is a unique work that combines shrewd philosophical ideas and rigorous arguments. It has influenced the development of metaphysics more than any other existing work of antiquity.* As it appeals to a range of thinkers from different cultural backgrounds and historical periods, Aristotle's text is likely to remain important. His notions such as "being qua being,"* substance, hylomorphism, and potentiality and actuality continue to re-emerge in philosophical debates to the present day. Historians of philosophy analyze these universally significant metaphysical ideas to gain a better understanding of their meaning and practicing philosophers have rediscovered them and given them new life by using them in cutting-edge arguments. The depth of its arguments and the complexity of its ideas suggest that Aristotle's *Metaphysics* has the potential to be found relevant to a wide range of philosophical debates that may emerge in the future.

NOTES

1   Jonathan Barnes, *A Very Short Introduction to Aristotle* (Oxford: Oxford University Press, 2000), 136.

2   Edward Feser, "Introduction: An Aristotelian Revival?" in *Aristotle on Method and Metaphysics*, ed. Edward Feser (New York: Palgrave Macmillan, 2013), 2.

3   Jonathan Beere, *Doing and Being: An Interpretation of Aristotle's Metaphysics Theta* (Oxford: Oxford University Press, 2009).

4   Aristotle, *Metaphysics: Books Zeta and Eta*, trans. with commentary David Bostock (Oxford: Clarendon Press, 1994).

5   Joshua Hoffman and Gary S. Rosenkrantz, *Substance: Its Nature and Existence* (London and New York: Routledge, 1997).

6   Tuomas Tahko, "Metaphysics as the First Philosophy," in *Aristotle on Method and Metaphysics*, ed. Edward Feser (New York: Palgrave Macmillan, 2013), 49–67.

GLOSSARY

GLOSSARY OF TERMS

Academy: philosophical school established by Aristotle's teacher Plato in the fourth century B.C.E.

Accidental property: a kind of property that is not essential to defining an object. For instance, a snub nose is an accidental property of a human being, because the shape of a nose varies from one person to another and thus it is not something that all humans fundamentally share.

Actuality: see Potentiality and actuality.

Analytic philosophy: branch of contemporary philosophy. Broadly speaking, the research methods of analytic philosophers differ from those of other philosophers with regard to their research methods—analytic philosophers base their research on logic and rigorous analysis.

Antiquity: the period before the Middle Ages, but within the span of Western human history.

Apeiron: a philosophical concept introduced by the pre-Socratic philosopher Anaximander. Literally meaning "limitless," it denotes the idea that a fundamental creative principle exists that has peculiar generative properties not resembling the properties of any familiar elements.

Athens: the center of Greek philosophical learning at the time of Aristotle; Athens is one of the oldest cities in the world and has been inhabited for at least seven thousand years.

Being qua being: a phrase introduced by Aristotle, best understood as "being by virtue of being." Aristotle used it to describe his inquiry into being. It refers to investigating what we would today call ontology.

Bundle theory: a metaphysical theory that suggests that objects are best understood as collections—"bundles"—of all the properties they possess. This is alternative to the view that objects have special substantial properties that determine their identity.

Christian: a person who believes in the religion of Christianity, based on the teachings of Jesus Christ.

Classical Greece: a period in Greek culture lasting for around 200 years, from the fifth to the fourth century B.C.E.

Cosmology: study of the universe as a whole; in the context of ancient philosophy, it refers to the question of the origin of the world, the primary forces that are active in the world, and so on.

Early modern period: the period of history following the late Middle Ages, from around 1500 C.E. to around 1800 C.E.

Empiricism: the belief that knowledge is obtained on the basis of experience and observation.

Enlightenment: eighteenth-century intellectual movement marked by an emphasis on reason and a rejection of tradition.

Essentialism: the view that objects have certain core properties or characteristics that make up their identity.

Exegesis: the critical analysis and interpretation of a text.

Hellenistic period: the three centuries between the death of Alexander the Great and the rise of the ancient Roman Empire. This period is accepted as being between 323 B.C.E. and 31 B.C.E.

Hylomorphism: term that refers to the idea that substance is a form present in matter. Aristotle was the first to introduce this idea.

Immanent form: a form present in matter, as opposed to an independently existing form. Aristotle was the first to propose a theory involving this notion.

Incorporeal: an adjective that describes an object that has no physical body.

Islam: a religion whose followers worship Allah as the only God and believe in the prophet Muhammad.

Logos: a very popular—and notoriously hard to translate—concept among ancient philosophers. It typically refers to rationality of either a person or even the world itself. It plays a very important role in the thought of the pre-Socratic Greek philosopher Heraclitus, who argued that logos was the forming principle of the world.

Lyceum: philosophical school established by Aristotle in Athens in the fourth century B.C.E. Members of this school are known as Peripatetics.

Macedonia: a kingdom on the northern edge of Classical Greece. It was the birthplace of Aristotle and Alexander the Great, who became its king.

Medieval period: also known as the Middle Ages, it is the period in European history that lasted from the fifth century C.E. to the fifteenth century C.E.

Metaphysics: subfield of philosophy that addresses the questions pertinent to existence, reality, or being itself.

Metic: term used to describe the social and political status of a person who resided in ancient Athens but was not a full citizen. Unlike citizens, metics could only partially participate in the political life, could not own land, and paid additional taxes.

Middle Ages: the period in European history that lasted from the fifth century C.E. to the fifteenth century C.E.

Milesian school: the earliest Greek school of thought, named after the town where it was founded (Miletus). The best-known members are Thales, Anaximander, and Anaximenes.

Neoplatonists: members of the Neoplatonic school of thought as established by Plotinus.

Ontology: subfield of metaphysics; it addresses questions relating to existence, such as "What exists in the world?," "What types of existence are there?," and "How can existences be grouped?"

Partaking: a standard philosophical term to describe how objects in the actual world interact with forms.

Peripatetics: the followers of Aristotle. It is said they were so named because the word derives from the Greek word for "walk" as Aristotle liked to walk around while he was delivering his lectures.

Platonic: relating to the work and thought of Plato.

Platonism: the philosophy of Plato.

Potentiality and actuality: Aristotelian concepts referring to modal states of objects. Potentiality refers to a possibility or capacity to change in a certain way, while actuality refers to the state when the capacity to change is fulfilled. An acorn, for instance, is potentially an oak tree, but an oak tree exists as an actual substance.

Pre-Socratics: large group of Greek philosophers active before and during Socrates' lifetime (around 469 B.C.E. to 399 B.C.E.). These philosophers held very diverse views and are sometimes grouped into different schools, but they shared an interest in metaphysics and natural science.

Renaissance: meaning "rebirth," the period of history from the fourteenth to the seventeenth century C.E., marked by a revival of art and literature in Europe.

Roman: relating to the ancient Roman civilization that began on the Italian peninsula as early as the eighth century B.C.E. and lasted until the fifth century C.E. At the height of its power and influence in the first and second centuries C.E. it expanded to become an empire covering 6.5 million square kilometers (or 2.5 million square miles).

Stoics: an ancient philosophical school. The Stoics are especially famous for their radical ethical views, although they also presented a number of important metaphysical and epistemological arguments.

Substance: a philosophical concept denoting an object's essence, which differs from any accidental properties the object might have.

The proponents of substance theory believe that the substance of a person is distinct, for instance, from that person being pale or having a snub nose. According to Aristotle, substance is an immanent form: that is, a form present in matter.

Substantial property: the kind of property that is essential to defining an object. A substantial property of a human being would be something that all human beings share and which is necessary for being human.

Theory of Forms: a theory that states that for every class of properties there is a universal form—an eternal, incorporeal entity that exists outside the actual world—which is both a perfect instance of that property and a cause of the existence of that property. For instance, human beings share the common property of being human in virtue of "partaking" in the Form of a Human Being.

Third man argument: an argument put forward by Aristotle that criticizes Plato's Theory of Forms. It shows that the forms cannot be the universals as their own existence calls for a universal.

Universal: a philosophical concept denoting certain general common characteristics shared by all objects of the same kind. Its opposite is a particular, which refers to a specific individual of that kind. For instance, your pet dog is a particular instance of the universal "dog."

Unmoved mover: according to Aristotle this mover is the first cause of all change in the universe. It causes motion, but is not itself moved by any previous action. Aristotle considers whether there are many unmoved movers or just one, but his conclusion remains unclear.

PEOPLE MENTIONED IN THE TEXT

John Ackrill (1921–2007) was a British classicist and philosopher. He produced several important studies on Aristotle's philosophy.

Alexander the Great (356–323 B.C.E.) was a Macedonian king. He is best known for his vast military conquests. At its height, his empire stretched from the eastern part of the Mediterranean to the Himalayas.

Alexander of Aphrodisias was a Peripatetic commentator and philosopher who was active around the turn of the third century C.E. He is best known for writing commentaries on various works by Aristotle.

Anaximander (c. 610–c. 546 B.C.E.) was one of the Pre-Socratics in the Milesian school. He is best known for introducing the theory of apeiron ("limitless"), which suggests that the world is generated by an element-like entity not resembling any ordinary elements.

Anaximenes (c. 585–c. 528 B.C.E.) was one of the pre-Socratics in the Milesian school. He is best known for arguing that air was the foundational principle and material of the world.

Andronicus of Rhodes was a Peripatetic philosopher who is best known for editing and publishing Aristotle's works in the first century B.C.E. Very little is known about Andronicus himself and only fragments of his own works survive.

Thomas Aquinas (1225–74 C.E.) was one of the most important medieval philosopher-theologians. He wrote on most areas of philosophy, from metaphysics to ethics. His most famous works are *Summa Theologica* and *Summa contra Gentiles*.

Averroes (Ibn Rushd) (1126–98 c.e.) was an Islamic philosopher especially known for his commentaries on Aristotle.

Avicenna (Ibn Sīnā) (980–1037 c.e.) was a Persian philosopher and intellectual. He is especially well known for contributing to the development of medicine, but his philosophical work is also substantial. His ontological theories about being were strongly influenced by Aristotle.

Jonathan Barnes (b. 1942) is an emeritus professor of philosophy at the University of Oxford. He is one of the best-known contemporary experts of ancient philosophy and has published numerous works on many ancient philosophers.

Jonathan Beere is a professor of ancient philosophy and history of science at the Humboldt-Universität zu Berlin. He specializes in ancient philosophy and has published a number of works on Aristotle's *Metaphysics*.

David Bostock (b. 1936) is an emeritus professor of philosophy at the University of Oxford. He has published many works on ancient philosophy, especially Plato and Aristotle.

Baruch Brody (b. 1943) is a professor of philosophy at Rice University in Texas. He is best known for his work in ethics, especially biomedical ethics.

Thomas Case (1844–1925) was a professor of moral and metaphysical philosophy at the University of Oxford. He is best known for his work in contemporary metaphysics, but he also produced several works on Aristotle.

S. Marc Cohen is an emeritus professor of philosophy at the University of Washington. He is an expert on ancient philosophy and has published many works on Aristotle.

Demosthenes (384–322 B.C.E.) was an orator and statesman in ancient Athens. He is especially well known for his political speeches.

Empedocles (490–430 B.C.E.) was a pre-Socratic philosopher and author of many notable doctrines. He is best known for being the first to advocate the four-element theory (fire, water, earth, air).

Edward Feser (b. 1968) is an associate professor of philosophy at Pasadena City College in Pasadena, California. He has published on a wide variety of topics in historical and contemporary philosophy.

Lloyd Gerson is a professor of philosophy at the University of Toronto. He is a noted expert who has published on many different topics in ancient philosophy.

Ilsetraut Hadot is an emerita professor at the French National Center for Scientific Research. She has published many works on ancient philosophy, especially Neoplatonism.

Verity Harte is a professor of philosophy and classics at Yale University. She is a specialist in ancient philosophy, with particular interest in Plato and Aristotle.

Heraclitus (535–475 B.C.E.) was one of the best-known pre-Socratics. He argued that the world is governed by logos, a kind of rationality which he likened to fire.

Joshua Hoffman is a professor of philosophy at the University of North Carolina at Greensboro. He is known for his work on metaphysics and theology.

David Hume (1711–76) was an important Scottish philosopher, especially known for his philosophical empiricism, the main belief of which is that the principal source of knowledge is the senses.

Terence Irwin (b. 1947) is a professor of ancient philosophy at the University of Oxford. He is an expert on ancient philosophy and the history of ethics.

Anthony Kenny (b. 1931) is an emeritus professor of philosophy at the University of Oxford. He is a noted expert on ancient philosophy and Aristotle.

Claude Panaccio (b. 1946) is a professor of philosophy at the University of Quebec. He is an expert in medieval philosophy.

Parmenides (late sixth or early fifth century B.C.E.) was a pre-Socratic philosopher, the founder of the Eleatic school of philosophy. He is known for the controversial theory of reality found in his fragmentary poem "On Nature."

Plato (429–347 B.C.E.) was a Greek philosopher who is one of the most important figures in the history of philosophy. His best-known works are the dialogues *Republic*, *Timaeus*, and *Apology*.

Plotinus (204–70 C.E.) was the founder of the Neoplatonic philosophical school. He is known for creating a complex but well-rounded philosophical system preserved in a work called *Enneads*.

Gary Rosenkrantz is a professor of philosophy at the University of North Carolina at Greensboro. He is known for his work on metaphysics and theological issues.

Theodore Scaltsas (b. 1949) is a professor of philosophy at the University of Edinburgh. He works on ancient philosophy and contemporary metaphysics.

David Sedley (b. 1947) is a professor of ancient philosophy at the University of Cambridge. He is a very well-known scholar who has worked on many areas of ancient philosophy.

Robert Sharples (1949–2010) was a professor in the Greek and Latin department at University College London during an extensive career and was well-respected for his work on Ancient Greek philosophy.

Christopher Shields is a professor of philosophy at the University of Notre Dame. He is an expert on ancient philosophy and has written extensively on Aristotle.

Socrates (470/469–399 B.C.E.) was a Greek philosopher, and one of the most important figures in the Western philosophical tradition. He is known for his rigorous philosophical questioning methods and interest in ethical questions. Socrates left no written works, so all we know of him comes from the writing of his pupils, most notably Plato.

Tuomas Tahko is an associate professor of philosophy at the University of Helsinki. He specializes in contemporary metaphysics.

Thales (c. 624–c. 546 B.C.E.) was one of the pre-Socratics in the Milesian school, typically referred to as the first philosopher in the Greek tradition. He is best known for arguing that water was the founding principle and material of the world.

WORKS CITED

WORKS CITED

Ackrill, J. L. *Aristotle the Philosopher*. Oxford: Oxford University Press, 1981.

Annas, Julia. *Ancient Philosophy: A Very Short Introduction*. Oxford: Oxford University Press, 2000.

Aristotle. *Categories*. Translated by John L. Ackrill. In vol. 1 of *The Complete Works of Aristotle: The Revised Oxford Translation*, edited by Jonathan Barnes, 3–24. Princeton, NJ: Princeton University Press, 1984.

Metaphysics. Translated by William David Ross. In vol. 2 of *The Complete Works of Aristotle: The Revised Oxford Translation*, edited by Jonathan Barnes, 1552–728. Princeton, NJ: Princeton University Press, 1984.

Metaphysics: Books Gamma, Delta, and Epsilon. Translated with notes by Christopher Kirwan. Oxford: Clarendon Press, 1993.

Metaphysics: Books Zeta and Eta. Translated with a commentary by David Bostock. Oxford: Clarendon Press, 1994.

Barnes, Jonathan. *A Very Short Introduction to Aristotle.* Oxford: Oxford University Press, 2000.

"Life and work." In *The Cambridge Companion to Aristotle*, edited by Jonathan Barnes,1–26. Cambridge: Cambridge University Press, 1995.

"Metaphysics." In *The Cambridge Companion to Aristotle*, edited by Jonathan Barnes, 66–108. Cambridge: Cambridge University Press, 1995.

"Roman Aristotle." In *Philosophia Togata* II, *Plato and Aristotle at Rome*, edited by Jonathan Barnes and Miriam Griffin. Oxford: Clarendon Press, 1997.

Beere, Jonathan. *Doing and Being: An Interpretation of Aristotle's Metaphysics Theta.* Oxford: Oxford University Press, 2009.

Bradley, F. H. *Appearance and Reality: A Metaphysical Essay*. London: S. Sonnenschein; New York: Macmillan, 1893.

Case, Thomas. "Aristotle." In *Aristotle's Philosophical Development: Problems and Prospects*, edited by William Wians, 1–40. Lanham, MD: Rowman & Littlefield, 1996.

Code, Alan. "Aristotle's Logic and Metaphysics." In *Routledge History of Philosophy, Volume II: From Aristotle to Augustine*, edited by David Furley, 40–75. London: Routledge, 1999.

Cohen, S. Marc. "Substances." In *A Companion to Aristotle*, edited by Georgios Anagnostopoulos, 197–213. Malden, MA: Wiley-Blackwell, 2009.

Feser, Edward. "Introduction: An Aristotelian Revival?" *In Aristotle on Method and Metaphysics*, edited by Edward Feser, 1–6. New York: Palgrave Macmillan, 2013.

Furley, David. Introduction to *Routledge History of Philosophy, Volume II: From Aristotle to Augustine*, edited by David Furley, 1–8. London: Routledge, 1999.

Gerson, Lloyd. *Plotinus*. London and New York: Routledge, 1994.

Guthrie, W. K. C. *The Greek Philosophers: From Thales to Aristotle*. London: Routledge, 2013.

Hadot, Ilsetraut. "The Role of the Commentaries on Aristotle in the Teaching of Philosophy According to the Prefaces of the Neoplatonic Commentaries on the *Categories*." *Oxford Studies of Ancient Philosophy* supplementary volume (1991): 175–89.

Harte, Verity. "Plato's Metaphysics." In *The Oxford Handbook of Plato*, edited by Gail Fine, 191–216.Oxford: Oxford University Press, 2008.

Hoffman, Joshua, and Gary S. Rosenkrantz. *Substance: Its Nature and Existence*. London and New York: Routledge, 1997.

Huggett, Nick. "Zeno's Paradoxes." *Stanford Encyclopedia of Philosophy*. Accessed February 11, 2015. http://plato.stanford.edu/entries/paradox-zeno/.

Irwin, Terence. "Aristotle." In *The Shorter Routledge Encyclopedia of Philosophy*, edited by Edward Craig, 50–67. London: Routledge, 2005.

Irwin, Terence, and Gail Fine. *Aristotle: Introductory Readings*. Indianapolis, IN: Hackett Publishing Company, 1996.

Kenny, Anthony. *Ancient Philosophy: A New History of Western Philosophy*. Oxford: Oxford University Press, 2006.

Kretzmann, Norman, and Eleonore Stump. "Thomas Aquinas." In *The Shorter Routledge Encyclopedia of Philosophy*, edited by Edward Craig, 30–48. London: Routledge, 2005.

Lear, Jonathan. *Aristotle: The Desire to Understand*. Cambridge: Cambridge University Press, 1988.

Loux, Michael. *Primary "Ousia": An Essay on Aristotle's Metaphysics Z and H*. Ithaca, NY: Cornell University Press, 1991.

Panaccio, Claude. "Medieval Metaphysics 1: The Problem of Universals." In *The Routledge Companion to Metaphysics*, edited by Robin Le Poidevin, Peter Simons, Andrew McGonigal, and Ross P. Cameron, 48–57. London and New York: Routledge, 2009.

Plato. *Phaedo*. Translated by G. M. A. Grube. In *Plato: Complete Works*, edited by John M. Cooper, 49–100. Indianapolis, IN; Cambridge: Hackett Publishing Company, 1997.

Sophist. Translated by Nicholas P. White. In *Plato: Complete Works*, edited by John M. Cooper, 235–293. Indianapolis, IN; Cambridge: Hackett Publishing Company, 1997.

Rizvi, Sajjad H. "Avicenna (Ibn Sīnā)." Internet Encyclopedia of Philosophy. Accessed February 11, 2015. http://www.iep.utm.edu/avicenna/.

Robinson, Howard. "Substance." *Stanford Encyclopedia of Philosophy.* Accessed February 10, 2015. http://plato.stanford.edu/entries/substance/.

Sachs, Joe. "Aristotle: Metaphysics." Internet Encyclopedia of Philosophy. Accessed February 10, 2015. http://www.iep.utm.edu/aris-met/.

Scaltsas, Theodore. *Substances and Universals in Aristotle's Metaphysics*. New York: Cornell University Press, 1994.

Sharples, Robert. "The Peripatetic School." In *Routledge History of Philosophy, Volume II: From Aristotle to Augustine*, edited by David Furley, 147–87. London and New York: Routledge, 1999.

Shields, Christopher. *Aristotle*. London: Routledge, 2007.

"Aristotle." *Stanford Encyclopedia of Philosophy*. Accessed February 10, 2015. http://plato.stanford.edu/entries/aristotle/.

"Aristotle's Philosophical Life and Writing." In *The Oxford Handbook of Aristotle*, edited by Christopher Shields, 3–16. Oxford: Oxford University Press, 2012.

Tahko, Tuomas. "Metaphysics as the First Philosophy." In *Aristotle on Method and Metaphysics*, edited by Edward Feser, 49–67. New York: Palgrave Macmillan, 2013.

Thom, Paul. "Logical Form." In *The Oxford Handbook of Medieval Philosophy*, edited by John Marenbon, 271–88. Oxford: Oxford University Press, 2012.

THE MACAT LIBRARY
BY DISCIPLINE

The Macat Library By Discipline

AFRICANA STUDIES

Chinua Achebe's *An Image of Africa: Racism in Conrad's Heart of Darkness*
W. E. B. Du Bois's *The Souls of Black Folk*
Zora Neale Huston's *Characteristics of Negro Expression*
Martin Luther King Jr's *Why We Can't Wait*
Toni Morrison's *Playing in the Dark: Whiteness in the American Literary Imagination*

ANTHROPOLOGY

Arjun Appadurai's *Modernity at Large: Cultural Dimensions of Globalisation*
Philippe Ariès's *Centuries of Childhood*
Franz Boas's *Race, Language and Culture*
Kim Chan & Renée Mauborgne's *Blue Ocean Strategy*
Jared Diamond's *Guns, Germs & Steel: the Fate of Human Societies*
Jared Diamond's *Collapse: How Societies Choose to Fail or Survive*
E. E. Evans-Pritchard's *Witchcraft, Oracles and Magic Among the Azande*
James Ferguson's *The Anti-Politics Machine*
Clifford Geertz's *The Interpretation of Cultures*
David Graeber's *Debt: the First 5000 Years*
Karen Ho's *Liquidated: An Ethnography of Wall Street*
Geert Hofstede's *Culture's Consequences: Comparing Values, Behaviors, Institutes and Organizations across Nations*
Claude Lévi-Strauss's *Structural Anthropology*
Jay Macleod's *Ain't No Makin' It: Aspirations and Attainment in a Low-Income Neighborhood*
Saba Mahmood's *The Politics of Piety: The Islamic Revival and the Feminist Subject*
Marcel Mauss's *The Gift*

BUSINESS

Jean Lave & Etienne Wenger's *Situated Learning*
Theodore Levitt's *Marketing Myopia*
Burton G. Malkiel's *A Random Walk Down Wall Street*
Douglas McGregor's *The Human Side of Enterprise*
Michael Porter's *Competitive Strategy: Creating and Sustaining Superior Performance*
John Kotter's *Leading Change*
C. K. Prahalad & Gary Hamel's *The Core Competence of the Corporation*

CRIMINOLOGY

Michelle Alexander's *The New Jim Crow: Mass Incarceration in the Age of Colorblindness*
Michael R. Gottfredson & Travis Hirschi's *A General Theory of Crime*
Richard Herrnstein & Charles A. Murray's *The Bell Curve: Intelligence and Class Structure in American Life*
Elizabeth Loftus's *Eyewitness Testimony*
Jay Macleod's *Ain't No Makin' It: Aspirations and Attainment in a Low-Income Neighborhood*
Philip Zimbardo's *The Lucifer Effect*

ECONOMICS

Janet Abu-Lughod's *Before European Hegemony*
Ha-Joon Chang's *Kicking Away the Ladder*
David Brion Davis's *The Problem of Slavery in the Age of Revolution*
Milton Friedman's *The Role of Monetary Policy*
Milton Friedman's *Capitalism and Freedom*
David Graeber's *Debt: the First 5000 Years*
Friedrich Hayek's *The Road to Serfdom*
Karen Ho's *Liquidated: An Ethnography of Wall Street*

John Maynard Keynes's *The General Theory of Employment, Interest and Money*
Charles P. Kindleberger's *Manias, Panics and Crashes*
Robert Lucas's *Why Doesn't Capital Flow from Rich to Poor Countries?*
Burton G. Malkiel's *A Random Walk Down Wall Street*
Thomas Robert Malthus's *An Essay on the Principle of Population*
Karl Marx's *Capital*
Thomas Piketty's *Capital in the Twenty-First Century*
Amartya Sen's *Development as Freedom*
Adam Smith's *The Wealth of Nations*
Nassim Nicholas Taleb's *The Black Swan: The Impact of the Highly Improbable*
Amos Tversky's & Daniel Kahneman's *Judgment under Uncertainty: Heuristics and Biases*
Mahbub Ul Haq's *Reflections on Human Development*
Max Weber's *The Protestant Ethic and the Spirit of Capitalism*

FEMINISM AND GENDER STUDIES

Judith Butler's *Gender Trouble*
Simone De Beauvoir's *The Second Sex*
Michel Foucault's *History of Sexuality*
Betty Friedan's *The Feminine Mystique*
Saba Mahmood's *The Politics of Piety: The Islamic Revival and the Feminist Subject*
Joan Wallach Scott's *Gender and the Politics of History*
Mary Wollstonecraft's *A Vindication of the Rights of Woman*
Virginia Woolf's *A Room of One's Own*

GEOGRAPHY

The Brundtland Report's *Our Common Future*
Rachel Carson's *Silent Spring*
Charles Darwin's *On the Origin of Species*
James Ferguson's *The Anti-Politics Machine*
Jane Jacobs's *The Death and Life of Great American Cities*
James Lovelock's *Gaia: A New Look at Life on Earth*
Amartya Sen's *Development as Freedom*
Mathis Wackernagel & William Rees's *Our Ecological Footprint*

HISTORY

Janet Abu-Lughod's *Before European Hegemony*
Benedict Anderson's *Imagined Communities*
Bernard Bailyn's *The Ideological Origins of the American Revolution*
Hanna Batatu's *The Old Social Classes And The Revolutionary Movements Of Iraq*
Christopher Browning's *Ordinary Men: Reserve Police Batallion 101 and the Final Solution in Poland*
Edmund Burke's *Reflections on the Revolution in France*
William Cronon's *Nature's Metropolis: Chicago And The Great West*
Alfred W. Crosby's *The Columbian Exchange*
Hamid Dabashi's *Iran: A People Interrupted*
David Brion Davis's *The Problem of Slavery in the Age of Revolution*
Nathalie Zemon Davis's *The Return of Martin Guerre*
Jared Diamond's *Guns, Germs & Steel: the Fate of Human Societies*
Frank Dikotter's *Mao's Great Famine*
John W Dower's *War Without Mercy: Race And Power In The Pacific War*
W. E. B. Du Bois's *The Souls of Black Folk*
Richard J. Evans's *In Defence of History*
Lucien Febvre's *The Problem of Unbelief in the 16th Century*
Sheila Fitzpatrick's *Everyday Stalinism*

Eric Foner's *Reconstruction: America's Unfinished Revolution, 1863-1877*
Michel Foucault's *Discipline and Punish*
Michel Foucault's *History of Sexuality*
Francis Fukuyama's *The End of History and the Last Man*
John Lewis Gaddis's *We Now Know: Rethinking Cold War History*
Ernest Gellner's *Nations and Nationalism*
Eugene Genovese's *Roll, Jordan, Roll: The World the Slaves Made*
Carlo Ginzburg's *The Night Battles*
Daniel Goldhagen's *Hitler's Willing Executioners*
Jack Goldstone's *Revolution and Rebellion in the Early Modern World*
Antonio Gramsci's *The Prison Notebooks*
Alexander Hamilton, John Jay & James Madison's *The Federalist Papers*
Christopher Hill's *The World Turned Upside Down*
Carole Hillenbrand's *The Crusades: Islamic Perspectives*
Thomas Hobbes's *Leviathan*
Eric Hobsbawm's *The Age Of Revolution*
John A. Hobson's *Imperialism: A Study*
Albert Hourani's *History of the Arab Peoples*
Samuel P. Huntington's *The Clash of Civilizations and the Remaking of World Order*
C. L. R. James's *The Black Jacobins*
Tony Judt's *Postwar: A History of Europe Since 1945*
Ernst Kantorowicz's *The King's Two Bodies: A Study in Medieval Political Theology*
Paul Kennedy's *The Rise and Fall of the Great Powers*
Ian Kershaw's *The "Hitler Myth": Image and Reality in the Third Reich*
John Maynard Keynes's *The General Theory of Employment, Interest and Money*
Charles P. Kindleberger's *Manias, Panics and Crashes*
Martin Luther King Jr's *Why We Can't Wait*
Henry Kissinger's *World Order: Reflections on the Character of Nations and the Course of History*
Thomas Kuhn's *The Structure of Scientific Revolutions*
Georges Lefebvre's *The Coming of the French Revolution*
John Locke's *Two Treatises of Government*
Niccolò Machiavelli's *The Prince*
Thomas Robert Malthus's *An Essay on the Principle of Population*
Mahmood Mamdani's *Citizen and Subject: Contemporary Africa And The Legacy Of Late Colonialism*
Karl Marx's *Capital*
Stanley Milgram's *Obedience to Authority*
John Stuart Mill's *On Liberty*
Thomas Paine's *Common Sense*
Thomas Paine's *Rights of Man*
Geoffrey Parker's *Global Crisis: War, Climate Change and Catastrophe in the Seventeenth Century*
Jonathan Riley-Smith's *The First Crusade and the Idea of Crusading*
Jean-Jacques Rousseau's *The Social Contract*
Joan Wallach Scott's *Gender and the Politics of History*
Theda Skocpol's *States and Social Revolutions*
Adam Smith's *The Wealth of Nations*
Timothy Snyder's *Bloodlands: Europe Between Hitler and Stalin*
Sun Tzu's *The Art of War*
Keith Thomas's *Religion and the Decline of Magic*
Thucydides's *The History of the Peloponnesian War*
Frederick Jackson Turner's *The Significance of the Frontier in American History*
Odd Arne Westad's *The Global Cold War: Third World Interventions And The Making Of Our Times*

LITERATURE

Chinua Achebe's *An Image of Africa: Racism in Conrad's Heart of Darkness*
Roland Barthes's *Mythologies*
Homi K. Bhabha's *The Location of Culture*
Judith Butler's *Gender Trouble*
Simone De Beauvoir's *The Second Sex*
Ferdinand De Saussure's *Course in General Linguistics*
T. S. Eliot's *The Sacred Wood: Essays on Poetry and Criticism*
Zora Neale Huston's *Characteristics of Negro Expression*
Toni Morrison's *Playing in the Dark: Whiteness in the American Literary Imagination*
Edward Said's *Orientalism*
Gayatri Chakravorty Spivak's *Can the Subaltern Speak?*
Mary Wollstonecraft's *A Vindication of the Rights of Women*
Virginia Woolf's *A Room of One's Own*

PHILOSOPHY

Elizabeth Anscombe's *Modern Moral Philosophy*
Hannah Arendt's *The Human Condition*
Aristotle's *Metaphysics*
Aristotle's *Nicomachean Ethics*
Edmund Gettier's *Is Justified True Belief Knowledge?*
Georg Wilhelm Friedrich Hegel's *Phenomenology of Spirit*
David Hume's *Dialogues Concerning Natural Religion*
David Hume's *The Enquiry for Human Understanding*
Immanuel Kant's *Religion within the Boundaries of Mere Reason*
Immanuel Kant's *Critique of Pure Reason*
Søren Kierkegaard's *The Sickness Unto Death*
Søren Kierkegaard's *Fear and Trembling*
C. S. Lewis's *The Abolition of Man*
Alasdair MacIntyre's *After Virtue*
Marcus Aurelius's *Meditations*
Friedrich Nietzsche's *On the Genealogy of Morality*
Friedrich Nietzsche's *Beyond Good and Evil*
Plato's *Republic*
Plato's *Symposium*
Jean-Jacques Rousseau's *The Social Contract*
Gilbert Ryle's *The Concept of Mind*
Baruch Spinoza's *Ethics*
Sun Tzu's *The Art of War*
Ludwig Wittgenstein's *Philosophical Investigations*

POLITICS

Benedict Anderson's *Imagined Communities*
Aristotle's *Politics*
Bernard Bailyn's *The Ideological Origins of the American Revolution*
Edmund Burke's *Reflections on the Revolution in France*
John C. Calhoun's *A Disquisition on Government*
Ha-Joon Chang's *Kicking Away the Ladder*
Hamid Dabashi's *Iran: A People Interrupted*
Hamid Dabashi's *Theology of Discontent: The Ideological Foundation of the Islamic Revolution in Iran*
Robert Dahl's *Democracy and its Critics*
Robert Dahl's *Who Governs?*
David Brion Davis's *The Problem of Slavery in the Age of Revolution*

The Macat Library By Discipline

Alexis De Tocqueville's *Democracy in America*
James Ferguson's *The Anti-Politics Machine*
Frank Dikotter's *Mao's Great Famine*
Sheila Fitzpatrick's *Everyday Stalinism*
Eric Foner's *Reconstruction: America's Unfinished Revolution, 1863-1877*
Milton Friedman's *Capitalism and Freedom*
Francis Fukuyama's *The End of History and the Last Man*
John Lewis Gaddis's *We Now Know: Rethinking Cold War History*
Ernest Gellner's *Nations and Nationalism*
David Graeber's *Debt: the First 5000 Years*
Antonio Gramsci's *The Prison Notebooks*
Alexander Hamilton, John Jay & James Madison's *The Federalist Papers*
Friedrich Hayek's *The Road to Serfdom*
Christopher Hill's *The World Turned Upside Down*
Thomas Hobbes's *Leviathan*
John A. Hobson's *Imperialism: A Study*
Samuel P. Huntington's *The Clash of Civilizations and the Remaking of World Order*
Tony Judt's *Postwar: A History of Europe Since 1945*
David C. Kang's *China Rising: Peace, Power and Order in East Asia*
Paul Kennedy's *The Rise and Fall of Great Powers*
Robert Keohane's *After Hegemony*
Martin Luther King Jr.'s *Why We Can't Wait*
Henry Kissinger's *World Order: Reflections on the Character of Nations and the Course of History*
John Locke's *Two Treatises of Government*
Niccolò Machiavelli's *The Prince*
Thomas Robert Malthus's *An Essay on the Principle of Population*
Mahmood Mamdani's *Citizen and Subject: Contemporary Africa And The Legacy Of Late Colonialism*
Karl Marx's *Capital*
John Stuart Mill's *On Liberty*
John Stuart Mill's *Utilitarianism*
Hans Morgenthau's *Politics Among Nations*
Thomas Paine's *Common Sense*
Thomas Paine's *Rights of Man*
Thomas Piketty's *Capital in the Twenty-First Century*
Robert D. Putman's *Bowling Alone*
John Rawls's *Theory of Justice*
Jean-Jacques Rousseau's *The Social Contract*
Theda Skocpol's *States and Social Revolutions*
Adam Smith's *The Wealth of Nations*
Sun Tzu's *The Art of War*
Henry David Thoreau's *Civil Disobedience*
Thucydides's *The History of the Peloponnesian War*
Kenneth Waltz's *Theory of International Politics*
Max Weber's *Politics as a Vocation*
Odd Arne Westad's *The Global Cold War: Third World Interventions And The Making Of Our Times*

POSTCOLONIAL STUDIES

Roland Barthes's *Mythologies*
Frantz Fanon's *Black Skin, White Masks*
Homi K. Bhabha's *The Location of Culture*
Gustavo Gutiérrez's *A Theology of Liberation*
Edward Said's *Orientalism*
Gayatri Chakravorty Spivak's *Can the Subaltern Speak?*

PSYCHOLOGY

Gordon Allport's *The Nature of Prejudice*
Alan Baddeley & Graham Hitch's *Aggression: A Social Learning Analysis*
Albert Bandura's *Aggression: A Social Learning Analysis*
Leon Festinger's *A Theory of Cognitive Dissonance*
Sigmund Freud's *The Interpretation of Dreams*
Betty Friedan's *The Feminine Mystique*
Michael R. Gottfredson & Travis Hirschi's *A General Theory of Crime*
Eric Hoffer's *The True Believer: Thoughts on the Nature of Mass Movements*
William James's *Principles of Psychology*
Elizabeth Loftus's *Eyewitness Testimony*
A. H. Maslow's *A Theory of Human Motivation*
Stanley Milgram's *Obedience to Authority*
Steven Pinker's *The Better Angels of Our Nature*
Oliver Sacks's *The Man Who Mistook His Wife For a Hat*
Richard Thaler & Cass Sunstein's *Nudge: Improving Decisions About Health, Wealth and Happiness*
Amos Tversky's *Judgment under Uncertainty: Heuristics and Biases*
Philip Zimbardo's *The Lucifer Effect*

SCIENCE

Rachel Carson's *Silent Spring*
William Cronon's *Nature's Metropolis: Chicago And The Great West*
Alfred W. Crosby's *The Columbian Exchange*
Charles Darwin's *On the Origin of Species*
Richard Dawkin's *The Selfish Gene*
Thomas Kuhn's *The Structure of Scientific Revolutions*
Geoffrey Parker's *Global Crisis: War, Climate Change and Catastrophe in the Seventeenth Century*
Mathis Wackernagel & William Rees's *Our Ecological Footprint*

SOCIOLOGY

Michelle Alexander's *The New Jim Crow: Mass Incarceration in the Age of Colorblindness*
Gordon Allport's *The Nature of Prejudice*
Albert Bandura's *Aggression: A Social Learning Analysis*
Hanna Batatu's *The Old Social Classes And The Revolutionary Movements Of Iraq*
Ha-Joon Chang's *Kicking Away the Ladder*
W. E. B. Du Bois's *The Souls of Black Folk*
Émile Durkheim's *On Suicide*
Frantz Fanon's *Black Skin, White Masks*
Frantz Fanon's *The Wretched of the Earth*
Eric Foner's *Reconstruction: America's Unfinished Revolution, 1863-1877*
Eugene Genovese's *Roll, Jordan, Roll: The World the Slaves Made*
Jack Goldstone's *Revolution and Rebellion in the Early Modern World*
Antonio Gramsci's *The Prison Notebooks*
Richard Herrnstein & Charles A Murray's *The Bell Curve: Intelligence and Class Structure in American Life*
Eric Hoffer's *The True Believer: Thoughts on the Nature of Mass Movements*
Jane Jacobs's *The Death and Life of Great American Cities*
Robert Lucas's *Why Doesn't Capital Flow from Rich to Poor Countries?*
Jay Macleod's *Ain't No Makin' It: Aspirations and Attainment in a Low Income Neighborhood*
Elaine May's *Homeward Bound: American Families in the Cold War Era*
Douglas McGregor's *The Human Side of Enterprise*
C. Wright Mills's *The Sociological Imagination*

Thomas Piketty's *Capital in the Twenty-First Century*
Robert D. Putman's *Bowling Alone*
David Riesman's *The Lonely Crowd: A Study of the Changing American Character*
Edward Said's *Orientalism*
Joan Wallach Scott's *Gender and the Politics of History*
Theda Skocpol's *States and Social Revolutions*
Max Weber's *The Protestant Ethic and the Spirit of Capitalism*

THEOLOGY

Augustine's *Confessions*
Benedict's *Rule of St Benedict*
Gustavo Gutiérrez's *A Theology of Liberation*
Carole Hillenbrand's *The Crusades: Islamic Perspectives*
David Hume's *Dialogues Concerning Natural Religion*
Immanuel Kant's *Religion within the Boundaries of Mere Reason*
Ernst Kantorowicz's *The King's Two Bodies: A Study in Medieval Political Theology*
Søren Kierkegaard's *The Sickness Unto Death*
C. S. Lewis's *The Abolition of Man*
Saba Mahmood's *The Politics of Piety: The Islamic Revival and the Feminist Subject*
Baruch Spinoza's *Ethics*
Keith Thomas's *Religion and the Decline of Magic*

COMING SOON

Chris Argyris's *The Individual and the Organisation*
Seyla Benhabib's *The Rights of Others*
Walter Benjamin's *The Work Of Art in the Age of Mechanical Reproduction*
John Berger's *Ways of Seeing*
Pierre Bourdieu's *Outline of a Theory of Practice*
Mary Douglas's *Purity and Danger*
Roland Dworkin's *Taking Rights Seriously*
James G. March's *Exploration and Exploitation in Organisational Learning*
Ikujiro Nonaka's *A Dynamic Theory of Organizational Knowledge Creation*
Griselda Pollock's *Vision and Difference*
Amartya Sen's *Inequality Re-Examined*
Susan Sontag's *On Photography*
Yasser Tabbaa's *The Transformation of Islamic Art*
Ludwig von Mises's *Theory of Money and Credit*

Macat Pairs

Analyse historical and modern issues from opposite sides of an argument. Pairs include:

HOW TO RUN AN ECONOMY

John Maynard Keynes's
The General Theory OF Employment, Interest and Money

Classical economics suggests that market economies are self-correcting in times of recession or depression, and tend toward full employment and output. But English economist John Maynard Keynes disagrees.

In his ground-breaking 1936 study *The General Theory*, Keynes argues that traditional economics has misunderstood the causes of unemployment. Employment is not determined by the price of labor; it is directly linked to demand. Keynes believes market economies are by nature unstable, and so require government intervention. Spurred on by the social catastrophe of the Great Depression of the 1930s, he sets out to revolutionize the way the world thinks

Milton Friedman's
The Role of Monetary Policy

Friedman's 1968 paper changed the course of economic theory. In just 17 pages, he demolished existing theory and outlined an effective alternate monetary policy designed to secure 'high employment, stable prices and rapid growth.'

Friedman demonstrated that monetary policy plays a vital role in broader economic stability and argued that economists got their monetary policy wrong in the 1950s and 1960s by misunderstanding the relationship between inflation and unemployment. Previous generations of economists had believed that governments could permanently decrease unemployment by permitting inflation—and vice versa. Friedman's most original contribution was to show that this supposed trade-off is an illusion that only works in the short term.

Macat analyses are available from all good bookshops and libraries.

Access hundreds of analyses through one, multimedia tool.
Join free for one month **library.macat.com**

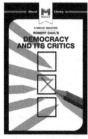

Macat Disciplines

Access the greatest ideas and thinkers across entire disciplines, including

TOTALITARIANISM

Sheila Fitzpatrick's, *Everyday Stalinism*
Ian Kershaw's, *The "Hitler Myth"*
Timothy Snyder's, *Bloodlands*

Macat Pairs

Analyse historical and modern issues from opposite sides of an argument. Pairs include:

RACE AND IDENTITY

Zora Neale Hurston's
Characteristics of Negro Expression

Using material collected on anthropological expeditions to the South, Zora Neale Hurston explains how expression in African American culture in the early twentieth century departs from the art of white America. At the time, African American art was often criticized for copying white culture. For Hurston, this criticism misunderstood how art works. European tradition views art as something fixed. But Hurston describes a creative process that is alive, ever-changing, and largely improvisational. She maintains that African American art works through a process called 'mimicry'—where an imitated object or verbal pattern, for example, is reshaped and altered until it becomes something new, novel—and worthy of attention.

Frantz Fanon's
Black Skin, White Masks

Black Skin, White Masks offers a radical analysis of the psychological effects of colonization on the colonized.

Fanon witnessed the effects of colonization first hand both in his birthplace, Martinique, and again later in life when he worked as a psychiatrist in another French colony, Algeria. His text is uncompromising in form and argument. He dissects the dehumanizing effects of colonialism, arguing that it destroys the native sense of identity, forcing people to adapt to an alien set of values—including a core belief that they are inferior. This results in deep psychological trauma.

Fanon's work played a pivotal role in the civil rights movements of the 1960s.

Macat analyses are available from all good bookshops and libraries.

Access hundreds of analyses through one, multimedia tool.
Join free for one month **library.macat.com**

Macat Pairs

Analyse historical and modern issues from opposite sides of an argument. Pairs include:

INTERNATIONAL RELATIONS IN THE 21ST CENTURY

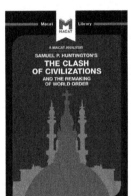

Samuel P. Huntington's
The Clash of Civilisations

In his highly influential 1996 book, Huntington offers a vision of a post-Cold War world in which conflict takes place not between competing ideologies but between cultures. The worst clash, he argues, will be between the Islamic world and the West: the West's arrogance and belief that its culture is a "gift" to the world will come into conflict with Islam's obstinacy and concern that its culture is under attack from a morally decadent "other."

Clash inspired much debate between different political schools of thought. But its greatest impact came in helping define American foreign policy in the wake of the 2001 terrorist attacks in New York and Washington.

Francis Fukuyama's
The End of History and the Last Man

Published in 1992, *The End of History and the Last Man* argues that capitalist democracy is the final destination for all societies. Fukuyama believed democracy triumphed during the Cold War because it lacks the "fundamental contradictions" inherent in communism and satisfies our yearning for freedom and equality. Democracy therefore marks the endpoint in the evolution of ideology, and so the "end of history." There will still be "events," but no fundamental change in ideology.